BELLE VUE

The Arts in Primary Education

Other titles from Bloomsbury Education

Education: A Manifesto for Change, by Richard Gerver

Leading on Pastoral Care, by Daniel Sobel

Wellbeing in the Primary Classroom: A practical guide to teaching happiness, by Adrian Bethune

Celebrating Difference: A whole-school approach to LGBT+ inclusion, by Shaun Dellenty

The Wellbeing Toolkit: Sustaining, supporting and enabling school staff, by Andrew Cowley

The Arts in Primary Education

Breathing life, colour and culture into the curriculum

Ghislaine Kenyon

BLOOMSBURY EDUCATION
LONDON OXFORD NEW YORK NEW DELHI SYDNEY

BLOOMSBURY EDUCATION
Bloomsbury Publishing Plc
50 Bedford Square, London, WC1B 3DP, UK

BLOOMSBURY, BLOOMSBURY EDUCATION and the Diana logo are
trademarks of Bloomsbury Publishing Plc

First published in Great Britain 2019

Text copyright © Ghislaine Kenyon, 2019

Ghislaine Kenyon has asserted her right under the Copyright, Designs and
Patents Act, 1988, to be identified as Author of this work.

Every reasonable effort has been made to trace copyright holders of material
reproduced in this book, but if any have been inadvertently overlooked the
publishers would be glad to hear from them.

Bloomsbury Publishing Plc does not have any control over, or responsibility
for, any third-party websites referred to or in this book. All internet addresses
given in this book were correct at the time of going to press. The author and
publisher regret any inconvenience caused if addresses have changed or sites
have ceased to exist, but can accept no responsibility for any such changes.

All rights reserved.
No part of this publication may be reproduced or transmitted in any form or
by any means, electronic or mechanical, including photocopying, recording, or
any information storage or retrieval system, without prior permission in writing
from the publishers.

A catalogue record for this book is available from the British Library.

ISBN: PB: 978-1-4729-6105-1; ePDF: 978-1-4729-6104-4; ePub: 978-1-4729-6103-7

2 4 6 8 10 9 7 5 3 1 (paperback)

Typeset by Newgen KnowledgeWorks Pvt. Ltd., Chennai, India
Printed and bound in India by Replika Press

All papers used by Bloomsbury Publishing Plc are natural, recyclable products
from wood grown in well-managed forests. The manufacturing processes
conform to the environmental regulations of the country of origin.

MIX
Paper from
responsible sources
FSC® C016779

To find out more about our authors and books visit www.bloomsbury.com
and sign up for our newsletters.

Contents

Acknowledgements vii

Introduction 1

Chapter 1 Why the arts should play a central role in primary schools   9

Chapter 2 Visual and plastic arts   17

Chapter 3 Music   43

Chapter 4 Dance   63

Chapter 5 Drama   77

Chapter 6 Literature: reading and writing it (and speaking it too!)   99

Afterword: The world in miniature – Windmill Hill Primary School   123

References   127
Index   131

Acknowledgements

At Bloomsbury, I thank Robin Baird-Smith for his heartening enthusiasm and my editor Hannah Marston for her encouragement and general steering; also for her generosity in understanding my need for illustrations.

I thank fellow writers, Mark Bostridge and Diane Samuels, who have been as supportive as they always are about my work.

Huge and sincere thanks go to all the headteachers, senior leaders, teachers, teaching assistants and admin staff who gave me their precious time, wisdom and organisational skills, in particular Katie Alexander, Rehana Ali, Ros Amber, Brian Anderson, Tess Bhesania, Tracy Bryden, Kate Condliffe, Penny Edwards, Kate Frood, Tessa Garland, Mark Hazzard, Naveed Idrees, Amy Nagla, Veena Naidoo, Juwon Ogungbe, Jimmy Rotheram, Nitsa Sergides, Anna Sutton and Kimberly Yate.

I thank all those professionals working independently or in arts organisations, and those working in education outside schools, for illuminating conversations and opportunities to see their work: Dal Babu, John Barber, Nadya Bettioui, Tori Drew, Nicola Freeman, Richard Frostick, Sean Gregory, Pat Hollister, Emily Jost, Caroline Kennedy, Johnny Langridge and colleagues, Neil MacGregor, Jenny Mollica, Jacqui O'Hanlon, Claire Pring, Ruth Sapsed, Jon Snow, Peter Wiegold and John Woolrich.

I thank Anna Bowman and Kornelia Cepok for their help in their respective archives and library.

For their help with sourcing and licensing the images, I'm very grateful to Christine Baker, Sir Quentin Blake, Dr Gabriele Finaldi, Sophie Greig, Mona Hatoum, Linda Kitson, Dominic Latham-Koenig, Elena Arevalo Melville, Catriona Smith, Emily Smith and Liz Williams.

I thank the many children whose work I was privileged to watch, whose faces and words proved and carry on proving to me what arts education really means.

I thank my husband Nick for supporting me while we were both writing books at the same time.

If I have not thanked you by name when I should have, I thank you now.

Introduction

Which experiences of your primary school years burn most brightly in your memory? Can you recall moments in your early education that helped you discover who you were? The you, that small person who already before the age of five had well-established preferences, interests, curiosity and budding abilities, and who went on to become the accomplished professional you are now. Think equally about the painful memories, of bullying teachers or peers, of tasks that were just too difficult, of the times when you were made to feel you'd failed, because of course those stand out too and have also formed you. Ask your colleagues these questions too; ask family and friends.

The answers to the first question are often the exceptional occasions: the residential trips where you had the most fun, being yourself outside the family borders, the trip to a museum or gallery where a window was opened for you into the past, as it was for TV historian Lucy Worsley when aged eight she saw and wondered delightedly about the Tudor toilets in Hampton Court, or the five-year-old Mary Beard's encounter with a 4,000-year-old piece of Egyptian cake in the British Museum. Or it was the time the owl man came into your school hall and you were first confronted with raw nature, a huge wild creature flapping loudly and thrillingly around the room, or the visiting drummers who turned the same familiar place into a new world of sounds and rhythms that unexpectedly reached deep into your core being. Perhaps it was the art lesson where you were given some different materials to experiment with: wonderfully malleable clay, a scratchy dip pen, jewel-coloured inks or thirsty watercolour paper and a tin of little watercolour pans. Or the day you discovered what a poem was: words, some new to you, some old friends, assembled in an entirely novel way, with a beat that made you feel something in a part of your body you didn't know you had. It could also of course have been a scientific experiment that did it for you, watching cream turn into butter, or the power of nature when you first saw a film of a volcanic eruption. Or it was that time when, sitting cross-legged on a carpet, you listened to Roald Dahl's *The Enormous Crocodile* and giggled at Quentin Blake's crazy drawings. And in all these cases, if it wasn't your parents, it was probably a good teacher who put such experiences in front of you, who led you.

Whichever it was for you, the memory of it has remained because it spoke directly to you; it reached inside you and found a sensitive spot, the one capable of responding to shape, colour, form, rhythm, melody, plot twists in a story or an experiment. Every one of those experiences has helped you become the person you are and who you are in the world. The more of these compelling, high-quality encounters children have at primary school, the more likely they are to be excited by and involved in their learning. This in turn helps them accept the necessary aspects of learning that appeal less directly.

This book argues that what are called the arts subjects – art, music and dance, drama and literature – have a unique ability to excite and motivate children because they are in themselves based on feelings; they are artists' own responses to their personal situation in the world. Sometimes these responses will be very close to the surface and obviously autobiographical – think of Michael Rosen's raw *Michael Rosen's Sad Book* about his reactions to the death from meningitis of his teenage son Eddie, or Van Gogh's frank and painful self-portrait with a bandaged ear, or Amy Winehouse's *Back to Black* album. But other life-responses will have been simmered and processed and distilled, or are too distant in time to be assessed in this way. Turner's *The Fighting Temeraire* is at first sight a painting about history – the moment when the now redundant warship famous for her performance in the Battle of Trafalgar is towed to her final resting place to be broken up. But it is also a work by an artist who was entering his own old age and at the same time perhaps reacting to the unwelcome pace of change around him. Yes, of course the way artists express and embody these feelings is highly skilled and based on countless hours of training and practice, but what we respond to is the way in which the original feelings of love, loss, joy and so on uniquely echo our own. Children without the baggage of respect for art are able to engage in a way that is genuine and direct – in fact they have a lot to teach us adults about that. And because they are also so in touch with their own feelings, they are also natural creators.

What we do with these responses to the arts can be complex, long-term and unpredictable. But years of research have shown that with young children, many of the skills and methodologies involved in arts learning and practice – collaboration, practice, playfulness, trying out, failing, succeeding – are not only essential life skills but also ones that lead to resilience in learning across the curriculum (see for example Arts Council England, 2014). Education policy has for its own reasons in the last few years increasingly marginalised these subjects by placing growing emphasis on maths and literacy, both in terms of curriculum time and, especially, in terms of assessment. For this reason, teachers are less and less trained to deliver the arts subjects in the classroom and training budgets are so often spent on assessment rather than on curriculum development. Consequently, and for the highly painful reason of budget cuts, many primary schools today have no arts specialists on the staff and the attention they feel able to pay to these foundation subjects is minimal and often tokenistic. Think about your own school. Perhaps you are an Artsmark or other arts-award school or you work with a local Bridge Connection, so you know the value of the arts, but you still keep them in an arts 'box' – an art week or a book week – which comes out once a term or once a year even.

And yet all across the country there are school leaders who have decided to hold on to the really broad curriculum that they know works for all children, and there are others who have courageously introduced one; and these schools succeed when they are judged by Ofsted (who have even been known to make a causal or at least an associative connection between curriculum and success in Ofsted criteria, as we'll see in the case study on page 86).

This book pays a visit to some of these schools and asks their leadership teams how and why they work in the way they do. It demonstrates that there are many delivery models and suggests that there will always be a way for you to include the arts in your school in a way that suits you and your governing body, and that even in times of biting budget cuts, data overload and pressures of assessment, it is possible to work in this rounded, inspiring and inclusive way. Many of my interviewees will say that it is much more than possible and that inclusion of the arts is an essential and integral ingredient of a successful school.

In this respect, we should also think about tradition and history. The educationist Robin Alexander (2001) has written powerfully about how deeply education systems are rooted in their own national cultures. When changes to an education system have been made as regularly and rapidly as they have been in England in the last 30 years, it is easy to be unaware of or forget earlier strands in English pedagogical practice. We are not a nation that has valued the arts in terms of public subsidy as much as say France and Germany have, but in the field of arts in primary education there has been a strong strand that has tapped into the ideas of Pestalozzi and Froebel about child-centred learning and enjoyment in learning involving art, music and creative play, for example (see www.jhpestalozzi.org and Froebel, 1895), which has in turn influenced the training of teachers if not always government policy. Since the 1920s at least there has been an unbroken line of advocates of a broad, creative and arts-rich approach to learning: William Hadow, Herbert Read, Sybil Marshall, Bridget Plowden, Alec Clegg and Ken Robinson are a few of the better-known names and there have been generations of teachers and schools in which their ideas have flourished. The arguments in favour of an arts-rich curriculum have changed over the years. The Plowden Report (Department of Education and Science, 1967) saw the arts as essential to building a healthy, socially just and democratic society; Alec Clegg, CEO for the West Riding of Yorkshire, 1945–74, encouraged teachers to use the arts as 'a means to strengthen identity and therefore social cohesion' (Burke, 2017); today, Darren Henley (current Chief Executive of Arts Council England) and others have stressed the economic argument that an arts education feeds the thriving creative industries (see for example Henley, 2016). The justifications may change and researchers will ask different questions, but the arts remain what they are and have always been: a dynamic agent for good in the primary school.

To return to my opening question about our experiences at primary school, I would like to add a word about myself. A few years ago I was commissioned to write the script for a documentary about a Victorian educationalist, Cornelia Connelly, who founded a teaching order of nuns, one of whose schools I went to as a child. The process of researching Connelly's life and ideas on how children are motivated to learn made me reflect on my own education at this school, and my conclusion was that the curriculum there may have been a little unusual at the time; and that my three stand-out and enduring memories of the positive kind were all arts-related. There were of course also negatives: I can't leave out the nun who never smiled and made me sit with a plate of cold, rubbery meat for hours until I finished it, or the sewing lesson, an activity I hated because I just couldn't grasp it – I recall my sweaty desperation as the thread became grubby and the finished piece increasingly elusive. But, in no special order, the three things that really made my heart beat faster were as follows. First, a song taught to us by a class teacher who also played the piano. I would have been five or six years old. The song was called 'Where'er You Walk' and I found out, as an adult, that it was from an opera called *Semele* by the 18th-century British-German composer Handel. The words go:

> *Where'er you walk*
> *Cool gales shall fan the glade*
> *Trees where you sit*
> *shall crowd into a shade*
> *Trees where you sit*
> *shall crowd into a shade*
> *Where'er you tread*
> *the blushing flowers shall rise*
> *and all things flourish*
> *and all things flourish*
> *Where'er you turn your eyes*

I still remember the feeling of hearing new words (glade, flourish) and new ideas (trees crowding) set to a rich new melody, and I can say now that I was *affected* by these things, that these words and that music had strange powers over me.

The second memory is of statues. The school was of course Catholic and in each classroom there was a statue of the Virgin Mary or Jesus or some other saint. These statues were mounted high up on the wall so they became a focal point, a distraction even. They were made of painted plaster, I imagine, but they were also clothed in what to my five-year-old eyes were beautifully unfamiliar fabrics, unlike anything my mother or her friends wore. There were satins and brocades and lace, in saturated colours: purples, greens and yellows; sometimes I would arrive on the first day of a new term and, as if by magic (or a miracle), the statue had been reclothed. Here I recall a sensual delight at seeing these smiling figures transformed by new colours and textures.

The last and most powerful memory is of a subject whose name (eurythmics) was too hard to pronounce, but the lesson itself was a longed-for weekly hour where the teacher played us extraordinary music on the piano or a recording, and, working in small groups, we were asked to invent and perform dance or movement narratives to it. We were offered bits of wonderful gauzy material (we could choose from a myriad of colours), which we could use to enhance the performance. The notion of inventing something together was of course not new – we did that when we played – but here we were also responding to music, a powerful external stimulus. We were responding with our whole bodies, our whole beings, and we were also doing so in a discipline; we were working within borders, including those of space and time. So there was a sense of shared achievement every time we figured out a series of movements that seemed to work; the experience was an unforgettable emotional takeover.

I can say with honesty that it was those particular elements – music, drama, visual art (and others like them) – experienced at an early age that made me buy into my education in general. It was worth coming to school to take part in those things and that then led me to do the things I ended up doing: primary teaching, as both class teacher with responsibility for art and music and then as deputy head; later, gallery-based education where, at the National Gallery and other places, I focused on visual art outside the classroom, and was able to train headteachers and teachers in using the arts as a stimulus for both subject and cross-curricular work. The results of this training have been expressed, for example, in the hundreds of schools from all over the country who take part so creatively in the National Gallery's Take One Picture scheme, which we started 20 years ago. At the Gallery, I also had the opportunity to work closely with Quentin Blake on various projects, including co-curating the exhibition 'Tell Me a Picture'; this collaboration, as well as many other artist contacts, stimulated my great interest in the way in which artists work, especially an artist of both words and pictures such as Blake, so I wrote a book on the subject called *Quentin Blake: In the Theatre of the Imagination*. It's this insight into both schools and the work of artists that has convinced me more than ever about how much an arts-rich curriculum can contribute to a school.

As teachers, we know that one of the most powerful motivations to learn is encouragement. So this book is also intended to be heartening – both bringing to the surface the part of you that is a creative human being and professional, and also offering you tried-and-tested strategies for doing the same in the staff and children you work with. Some or many of the elements will be familiar to you but this book is about working towards major change. Taking the leap to introduce a genuine arts-based curriculum into your school will involve you and the whole staff team in a working journey that will take time, training and probably much persuasion. But all my interviewees who have been on this adventure confirmed to me that every minute spent on it was repaid many times over in the children's and staff's enthusiasm, in improved attendance and behaviour and in a general sense of wellbeing. I have put this book together but the voices you will hear in it and the experiences described are largely those of school leaders and of arts professionals who partner with schools, from all around the country, who are doing extraordinary work in difficult times.

Bon courage (the French phrase for good luck, which is not about luck at all)!

Chapter 1
Why the arts should play a central role in primary schools

'A child's play is his work' (Friedrich Froebel, 1895)

In this chapter, we will explore why the arts are so important in primary schools and why they must play a central role in our teaching. The chapter suggests that when artists develop and make their work, they are engaging in play. They are experimenting, testing theories and asking the 'what if' questions. This approach, as well as being fundamental to artistic creativity, applies to all learning in a beneficial way. There are no right or wrong answers in this approach, for example, which means that everyone has something to contribute. This builds children's confidence, leads to success and benefits our teachers' creativity too.

The arts are fundamentally about playing (the basis of all art)

'Tom liked to fool around. He fooled around with sticks and stones and crumpled paper, with mewses and passages and dustbins, with bent nails and broken glass and holes in fences.' From *How Tom Beat Captain Najork and His Hired Sportsmen* by Russell Hoban (2013); see Illustration 1.1 by Quentin Blake.

How Tom Beat Captain Najork and His Hired Sportsmen is one of its illustrator Quentin Blake's favourite texts for children. He loved making the drawings for many reasons but one was that, as a passionate educationist (and one-time teacher), he feels it's one of the best books about learning he has come across. What Tom is doing, Blake thinks, is learning in the best self-directed way, through imaginative and experimental play.

We have all been children but we may have forgotten the feelings associated with the ordinary moments of our young childhood: times when we were fooling about (playing) at home or outside, away from adults, either on our own or with siblings or friends. And yet, as we know, the significance of play can hardly be exaggerated. Not only is play comprehensively enjoyable but it is also part of learning how to be a grown-up adult. As psychologist Peter Gray (2013) puts it: 'Playing with other children [...] is how children learn to make their own decisions, control their emotions and impulses, see from others' perspectives, negotiate differences with others, and make friends [...] play is how children learn to take control of their lives.'

Gray defines play as something that:

1 is self-chosen and self-directed
2 is an activity in which means are more valued than ends
3 has structure or rules that are not dictated by physical necessity but emanate from the minds of the players
4 is imaginative, non-literal, mentally removed in some way from 'real' or 'serious' life
5 involves an active, alert but non-stressed frame of mind.

However, as this definition suggests, play can be about more than fostering these important life skills and learning to learn, as Quentin Blake feels. Watch a group of under-fives engaged in imaginative playing (sometimes called *sociodramatic* play) at home: a narrative is proposed, characters and props are needed to realise the story – a bed for a sick teddy bear to start with, so someone thinks of a cardboard box and runs off to find one. Another child suggests a towel for a sheet. The doctor wants a stethoscope: 'We could make one out of some string? But no! We could use those earphones', and they are away. In this created world, the drive to find the solutions to the needs of the narrative is absolute. They have set themselves a task and found themselves the answer using imagination as a tool. Another time a cardboard box can be a table, a chair, a boat or a castle, the towel a bride's veil, a tablecloth, a bandage or a flag. Everything is possible in this world. In fact the notion of play taking place in a space that is removed from real life, where the process itself is paramount, the principle of it being self-chosen and self-directed – these things also all underpin and underlie the way that most artists work. You could describe artists (in all the art forms) as people who have not unlearned playfulness and how to play.

Take Quentin Blake when he made those drawings for Captain Najork: for him the text was the starting point and then Blake fooled around in more or less the way that Tom does. Russell Hoban begins the story with the encouraging words, 'Tom liked to fool around. He fooled around with sticks and stones and crumpled paper.' Hoban doesn't tell us *how* Tom fooled around – here the visual artist (illustrator) starts playing and comes up with the little sculpture in the image. Blake's working methods are worth mentioning here too. He will fiddle about making roughs for the final image for that page. These roughs, as the word suggests, start as quickly scribbled little drawings in which the subject of the drawing (in this case Tom with the sticks and stones and paper) is imagined and laid out. There will often be several of these – the bins in his studio are usually overflowing by the end of a session – and finally one will be selected. But this is not the end of the process because there is still some imagining to do. Blake places the final drawing on a light box and lays a blank sheet of watercolour paper on top. The light penetrates and he sees through to the drawing underneath, but what he does next is not to trace it but rather use it as a kind of indication for the finished drawing. As he says, you can't quite see it properly. Even this finished drawing has a spontaneous feeling to it. At the end of the process Blake is still imagining and still admitting new possibilities or new feelings about the subject.

Of course, by the time Blake illustrated Captain Najork he was already a highly skilled draughtsman. He had put in Malcolm Gladwell's (2009) 10,000 hours of 'deliberate practice' (a concept whereby people who excel in a discipline have usually spent 10,000 hours learning and practising the necessary techniques). This included life-drawing, which enabled him to be in control of his technique. He didn't need to work out how to draw a boy with his head in one dustbin and his feet supporting him on another. But the inspiration for the idea for the drawing came from nowhere in particular, other than through fiddling about with the pen on paper until the right version arrived. The fiddling is not limited to the visual arts (or to music). As novelist Ben Okri (1997) wrote on the subject of creativity: 'Do not disdain the idle, strange, ordinary, nonsensical, or shocking thoughts which the mind throws up. Hold them. Look at them. Play with them.' Similarly, listen to the words of M. C. Escher (1989), the artist of those crazy staircases (search for *Relativity* and *House of Stairs*, for example): 'I can't keep from fooling around with our irrefutable certainties. It is, for example, a pleasure knowingly to mix up two and three dimensionalities, flat and spatial, and to make fun of gravity.'

So there's the playful kind of playing, and there's the daydreaming kind. Listen to Norman Ackroyd (2018), the 80-year-old artist and printmaker of atmospheric dark images of British islands and coasts, describing his inspiration: 'it's that wonderful lucid thing you get when you start daydreaming when you're just waking up, that's an image that can't be described – it's like trying to catch a butterfly, and it comes from memory'.

This is exactly the state of mind that Gray refers to in his fifth definition: play as involving 'an active, alert but non-stressed frame of mind'. Think about the ideas that come to you when you're on a solo walk or having a shower, away from the pressing concerns of work or family life, or the daydreaming, the times when your brain can make the random but fruitful connections we describe as creative. This non-stressed but alert state enables the playfulness so necessary to the making of art. Working from this playful start seems to help children's concentration: at Cleveland Road Primary School in Ilford, for example, there is a full-time dance teacher who is often asked by the class teachers to hold the dance lessons in the morning because the energy, the creative focus and the release of endorphins seem to lead to an attentive readiness for the subjects where different parts of the brain are engaged.

So children are creative when they are at their most alert, using a methodology of experimentation that is still natural to them; they are creative when they are handed an open-ended opportunity to make a sculpture, compose a piece of music, create a dance sequence, or perform in a play. They will of course need skills, some rules of the game, some limitations, but the thing they won't need to learn is the imaginative bit. And just as a successful bit of imaginative play is its own reward, arts activities are enjoyable, naturally expressive, fulfilling and therefore motivating for all kinds of learning.

There are no wrong answers in the arts

I recently watched a dance class at Cleveland Primary School. As part of a whole-school cross-curricular project on the First World War, a Year 3 class were developing a dance inspired by the work of war artist Linda Kitson (see Illustration 1.2).

Team-taught by the dance instructor Katie Alexander and the class teacher, the children were working in groups, creating movements that echoed Kitson's jagged lines and then performing them to each other. Each little sequence was based on a response – an emotional response – to those lines, which were themselves a response to the artist's strong feelings about being in the middle of a theatre of war. The children were purposeful, concentrated and demonstrated knowledge and skills in dance in the way that they used their bodies in space and time (they had had dance classes since Reception). As they presented their ideas back to each other, the dance instructor and the class teacher used dance vocabulary to describe their movements and made a point of emphasising the differences between each group's work. Afterwards Katie said to me, 'There are 35 children in this class; there's such a range of responses but we're all on the same level here, the class teacher, the LSA, the children and me, and that's why the arts are so accessible. They're a tool to reach all children and adults. Fundamentally I teach the same lesson to Reception and Year 6; it's just that the reactions are different.'

What Katie means is that the creative response to a stimulus – in this case the art – was personal, unique to that child, and uniquely valuable. Any one child's response was not worse or less valid than another child's or an adult's: there was no wrong answer to the question, 'How do you respond?' It was all material to be worked with. This will be developed in relation to dance in Chapter 4 (page 63).

So, there are no wrong answers in creation. The principle also applies to perceptions of art. When I work with children (or adults) in front of a painting or a sculpture, I often ask a starter question such as, 'What do you notice first in this work?' The question is intended principally to get the participants looking closely and to start decoding, but many years of doing this has taught me that what also happens is that personal response affects how people look at art. I once showed a group of children the painting known as 'The Arnolfini Portrait' by the 15th-century painter Jan Van Eyck (see Illustration 1.3). One child noticed the dog (she had a dog at home), another the shoes lying so prominently in the foreground on the left, another the woman's green dress (the child liked the colour), and yet another the unusual mirror in the centre. The children were all picking up on elements the artist had intended them to – elements that contribute to the meaning of the work – but they were prioritising the things that had meaning to them personally. Everyone had something to contribute. Teachers often say to me after these sessions that the children who are quick to spot things in works of art are frequently those who struggle with the more academic side of the curriculum.

The arts lead to success

If there are no wrong answers when it comes to ideas in the arts, then you have to be right, and being right is good for you, especially when you are a small, non-powerful person. When children are playing or creating something on their own or in a group, ideas can and should be refined and developed, sometimes with the help of teachers, but that initial thought or response belongs to its initiator alone. The validation by adults of these creative impulses in children is one of the key strands in this book, because, as we all know, success breeds confidence and the opposite is also true. At the National Gallery, I taught a Year 3 class in which a boy noticed something in a painting that was not usually remarked on. I can't remember what the detail was but I will never forget the confused but delighted look on his face when I thanked him for his intelligent response, and his words: 'No one has ever said that to me before, Miss.' The validation of that boy's response was also a validation of his person.

I recently evaluated a music education project, London Music Masters – Learning, which at the time took place in three London primary schools. The children were offered musicianship and violin tuition from Reception upwards and the programme led to various performance opportunities either at school or in venues such as the Southbank Centre or The Royal College of Music. Interviewing the children after the first year, I learned that the element of the programme they all valued most highly was not, as I had expected, learning a new skill, but instead it was 'being able to perform in front of my parents' and 'for my parents to see how well I was doing'.

Brian Anderson, Headteacher of Springhead Primary School in Stoke-on-Trent, where they have a major Shakespeare focus across the curriculum, told me about a Year 4 pupil, a boy with dyslexia who was afraid of writing and afraid of getting spellings and handwriting wrong. The class were working on *The Taming of the Shrew* and in a workshop session a phrase came up that the children needed to explore. The boy came up with an interesting and convincing suggestion. 'He wouldn't have said that in class,' Brian commented. 'Then when they did go back to the class to do some writing, all the children asked him, "What was that sentence you said?", and the boy sent his teaching assistant away and did the writing himself. He got a Level 4 (up from a 2 at the beginning of the year).' Through a success gained in the unpressured setting of a drama workshop where all possibilities were admitted, he'd got the confidence and self-belief to tackle something in the classroom he normally shunned.

The arts are also good for teachers

Teaching the arts can be challenging for many teachers. So many have had little or no training to deliver them. I have been involved in countless INSET sessions in art or music where teachers have been as reluctant to pick up a paintbrush or produce a singing voice as the boy with dyslexia had been to write in his workbook. The comments they make suggest to me that they are still feeling the ache of failure. Perhaps in their heads they are still the seven-year-old who has been told that their drawing is not realistic or that they are tone deaf. So teachers' confidence in the arts is an issue here but there may also be something about values.

Quentin Blake (2009) has a thought about what he calls the 'unidentical twins': 'the verbal and the visual skills'. These, he says, start out as identical: 'they're growing up together but when you reach a certain age, the visual one becomes worthless and is pushed to one side and the verbal one becomes important… that's the one that teaches you to get a job… how to fill in forms, but what's important is to get those in balance.' The notion of arts as something you might do in an arts week or as a treat further marginalises these visual skills, and may also make them appear unessential.

When teachers do manage to 'pick up the paintbrush', however, they very often surprise themselves, and the language of delight after they have dared to do so is revealing. 'I feel as if I've died and gone to heaven,' one said to me after a practical session in which she made a painting on wood, having cut the panel herself with a jigsaw, primed it and mixed tempera paints combining egg yolk with water and pigments. It seemed as if this might have been the first time in many years that this teacher had connected with her creative self and as a result she appeared to have a deeper understanding of the many-layered effects this kind of work might have on the learners in her class.

This book is therefore also about teachers' own creativity, not only practical – I have seen teachers printmaking, dancing, reciting poetry and singing alongside their classes – but especially also connected to the planning of an inventive and inspiring curriculum; many examples of this will be described in the following chapters.

The book is an argument then for the arts to be much more than a marginal part of the curriculum that needs to be ticked off a checklist, simply because it's there. It's about how and why the arts can be deeply baked into your primary curriculum. For a start, they help children discover their own passions and talents, they confirm and affirm the self, and, because they are about the whole self, they address and are available to all children (and staff) of all abilities and at all levels. There are many other benefits of a curriculum that is arts-rich, arts-based even, and these will emerge throughout the book. This is easy for me to say but as a school leader you will have big questions: how do we go about integrating the arts into our school given the demands of Ofsted, parents, governors and other stakeholders? Is there a best way to persuade everybody of the value of such a curriculum? How do we develop arts skills in our staff? And, most pressing perhaps, can we afford it when our budgets are so restricted that we're having to ask parents to pay for books and materials? The schools represented in this book, and hundreds of others that aren't, have answered these questions persuasively through their success. Watch them and listen to them.

Chapter 2
Visual and plastic arts

'I found I could say things with color and shapes that I couldn't say any other way – things I had no words for.' (Georgia O'Keeffe, 1926)

This chapter will explore the visual and plastic arts and how we can use them for learning opportunities in the primary classroom. We will look at illustration in existing resources such as picture books, free art available in public spaces and how we can make the most of local art galleries and museums.

Illustration: the art of pictures in books and other graphic places

The resources you need for an arts-rich and creative curriculum are probably already there in your school or neighbourhood: you may have staff members and parents with skills or talents you are unaware of, plenty of outside space, cupboards full of books and art materials, the glory of the internet, places to display work, accessible arts venues, and a town, village or natural environment on your doorstep. If you are thinking about developing a curriculum where the arts are truly embedded, you could start to look at these in-house things differently, see them with new eyes and ask what they can do for you.

Let's start with illustrated books, a resource you are absolutely certain to have, and see what the broader learning opportunities might be. Certainly we use them to encourage beginning readers, to entice children into books in the first place, but perhaps they can do much more for us. I'm beginning with illustration because it is the everyday art that we can all access. In fact it may be so familiar that we may not consider it as art at all. But think of all the 'fine' artists who have illustrated children books – David Hockney's *Six Fairy Tales from the Brothers Grimm,*

Peter Blake's *ABC* or his *Alice Through the Looking Glass*, Salvador Dalí's *Alice in Wonderland*, Andy Warhol's *Little Red Hen* – quite apart from the great artists who have stayed with the form of illustration, from John Tenniel and E.H. Shepard to Beatrix Potter, from Maurice Sendak and Eric Carle to Raymond Briggs and Lauren Child – and you realise what a complete and totally varied art form it can be. And if it's that serious then it deserves to be given the same attention as great texts. This also helps to make the point that we can use the same looking skills when we look at illustration as we do with art that might be considered more difficult or remote, and that works of art of all kinds can then be used in the classroom to start projects in many curriculum areas.

Illustrated books come in many and sophisticated forms and I suggest that they have a place in every primary classroom from Reception to Year 6. At their most basic they are books with pictures and no words – think David Wiesner's *Flotsam*, Aaron Becker's *Journey* series or Quentin Blake's *Clown*. At the next level are books with full-page colour illustrations and a line or two of text per page, such as Jan and Jerry Oke's *Naughty Bus*, Jon Klassen's *This Is Not My Hat* or the Cozy Classics edition of *Pride and Prejudice* with its single-word-per-page text. Then come illustrated chapter books, such as those by Roald Dahl or Chris Riddell with their black and white half- or quarter-page images, books for resilient readers with vignettes at the top of the page and of course, in a different category but totally dependent on images, the graphic novels, so popular with many children who struggle with reading. You will have your own favourites but perhaps you have focused on their relevance to the English or literacy curriculum. There are a myriad of online resources around illustrated texts for phonics, texts for vowels sounds, or for teaching narrative techniques. These books can also be used, as Michael Rosen (2017) has suggested in a tweet, to enable children to 'make cognitive leaps between text and picture as they figure out the relationship between word and image. This advances logic, perception and reason.' But what if we also look at them because of what the illustrations themselves have to offer?

In 2000 I co-curated an exhibition at the National Gallery with Quentin Blake called 'Tell Me a Picture' in which we selected 13 works from the National Gallery's collection (European paintings made between 1250 and 1900) and 13 examples of images by picture book illustrators. The numbers are relevant because the idea was to have each letter of the alphabet represented by one artist, and in this way for the exhibition to be a non-hierarchical exploration of how to look at pictures. So we had a work by Goya hanging next to one by Michael Foreman, and a drawing by Emma Chichester Clark, of *Blue Kangaroo* fame, next to a painting by 19th-century graphic artist Honoré Daumier. The works had no conventional museum labels but were linked by Blake's own drawings on the walls: a small gang of children zanily commenting on the works or asking questions about them, and so giving permission to visitors to join the conversation about the art (see Illustration 2.1).

Here it's important to say that Blake's choice of National Gallery pictures was unconventional. There were no obviously 'child-friendly' paintings and there were very few animals, children or pretty Impressionist landscapes. Instead, his guiding principle was to find works that, like the illustrations, had a sense of story, and some of those turned out to be unexpectedly dark.

However, we also set up a website where we invited young online visitors to tell their own stories about the images, which they did imaginatively, internationally and in great numbers, and it became clear that the dark pictures were as popular as the more cheerful ones. Over 250,000 people visited the exhibition over its six-month run and from them we learned that the experience of becoming involved in the images in your own way (rather than being told what to think by a museum label) was a liberating and joyful one for many people, and that it could be a stimulus for high-quality writing.

So with illustrated books, looking at and talking about images even before you start on the text can be a useful way to begin. You may find it easy to talk about texts because you already do so, but is there an appropriate framework to discuss illustration? I'm going to use two pictures from *The Long Slide* as an example. This book is now out of print, but the images, by artist Ray Smith, are deceptively simple, of very high quality and capable of encouraging especially productive discussion. Nevertheless, the point here is that this can be done with whichever picture book a teacher feels most comfortable with.

The Long Slide is a book with a succinct, line-per-page text, whose vocabulary has just the right number of unfamiliar words to make it memorable to an Early Years child and also a level of sophistication that would make it suitable for use throughout the primary school. The follow-up activities suggested on the next pages could work with a Year

6 class making a book for an Early Years class. As with all good picture books, the story of *The Long Slide* is a very simple one: three toys, Jacko, Teddy and Barley, take an extraordinary journey. In a field they notice a great ladder, which naturally they want to climb. It's a journey full of danger, deafening planes, passing witches, not to mention air-sickness. But there are treats too, wonderful views and the pleasure of tumbling down the longest slide anyone can imagine. The original images are made with different techniques and media: the fine and softly drawn pencil lines are appropriate for the gently extensive landscape or skies, while the harder, inked contours of the figures and the ladder give us another level of reality. The first image (Illustration 2.2) is a beautiful drawing of a cow completely ignoring the excitement and trepidation felt by the three toys setting out. It also subtly suggests the characters of the toys: Teddy, the leader, climbing ahead, Barley, the more timid one, almost being pushed up by the practically minded Jacko, carrying a handy rope and a backpack with the picnic. The second image (Illustration 2.3) is particularly apt for open questioning: what would it be like climbing that ladder when you see how high it is? What can you see in the clouds?

Talking about these images with children, factual information can be elicited through open questioning: 'What can you see?', 'What kind of place are the toys in?', 'How has the artist made the picture?' and 'What tools did (s)he use?' But to go back to our idea about playfulness, the discussion around the image is also an opportunity to get children engaging imaginatively with it. Asking, 'What might Barley be thinking?' encourages a child to *be* Barley, to be faced with something frightening but at the same time appealing in its strangeness. The text only hints at these ambivalent, subtle feelings but pictures can express them in a non-verbal and therefore more direct way. When you interrogate the image, then, you achieve at least two things. First you see how the text can be complemented by pictures: how pictures can say a little more than the words do and can be funnier, sadder, more complicit with the child perhaps. Second you see how they address the child directly, inspiring responses of empathy or imagination.

The words and feelings stimulated by reading and talking about picture books can be picked up and built on through practical activities. As suggested above, work with *The Long Slide* could lead to the creation of a class book by an older class for use in a younger one. The book could be a sequel to it, perhaps introducing three new toy characters who have an adventure with a different theme, such as *The Long Jump* or *The Long Swim*.

There would be art curriculum opportunities here: to teach drawing skills, for example, using different media to suggest different aspects of the images as Ray Smith did. Here you could either follow his example or choose two different techniques to suit your curriculum and resources. This could be linked to an English objective of developing narrative techniques or an art or geography focus relating to topographical features, either local or global. This approach is of course applicable to any good picture book and any age group. Here, there is often a question about whether picture books (as opposed to any other kinds of illustrated books) properly belong in Year 5 and 6 classrooms alongside novels and other forms, as much as in Years 2 and 3 and below. There are many ways to justify this, not just that the best ones are wonderful examples of visual art in themselves. Another reason is that so many, including *The Long Slide* just described, have highly sophisticated texts that older children can learn just as much from. A third reason is that for children who are undergoing all the pressures of growing up, anticipating the transition to secondary school (and not always with excitement), a much-loved picture book is a reassuring connection to the safe world of early childhood. At the same time, it's a kind of affirmation of the ten-year-old person the child has also become.

Alongside its place in books, illustration operates as visual communication in many other fields, including advertising and public information, where it has its own set of skills. Organisations such as London's House of Illustration offer INSET for teachers to develop these skills and apply them specifically to the classroom situation: whether to explain a science subject visually, to address a PSHCE (personal, social, health and citizenship education) topic such as diversity or healthy lifestyle, or to promote a school through a poster campaign. If you give illustration the attention it deserves, and get teachers and children thinking creatively together about it, there are no limits to where it can lead.

Noticing: free art in the public sphere

Picture books that you already own are an easy source of quality images, but you can also find the work of artists in the public sphere. See Illustration 2.4 for some examples. Artists have been involved in making work with and for communities for hundreds of years. Think of cave paintings, art in churches, public statues or outdoor sculpture – Dhruva Mistry's work in Victoria Square in Birmingham, for example – or any one of the many works in the Yorkshire Sculpture Park near Wakefield. Whether your school is in a rural village, a town or a large metropolis, there will be work by artists and designers, some of which will have been commissioned specifically to make the environment more attractive, lively or interesting for the people who live or work there. Such art is freely available and it's worth considering using it alongside other artworks when you are building up your art or perhaps your history resources. Some work in the public sphere will be big and well-known, such as Gateshead's *Angel of the North* by Antony Gormley, but there will be small things too: a doorway with a beautifully carved lintel, a really well-executed bit of graffiti (admittedly you may have some civic or legal contextualisation to do unless it's a Banksy…), or even an object that someone has proudly displayed in their front window for the benefit of passers-by, which can be just as rich for your purposes. The following paragraphs are designed to get you thinking about finding these things and about how they might be incorporated imaginatively into your curriculum.

Finding art and design in the environment is not hard but it does need a slow moment because some of it may be such a familiar feature of, say, your route to work or the shops that you may never have stopped to look at it or even recognised it for what it is. Illustration 2.4 gives you an idea of the range of possibilities, and of course you can do online research. By far the most creative and enjoyable solution, though, would be for you and your staff to use an INSET planning session to take a walk in your locality and see what you can find: a wall painting in a village church, a war memorial, a print in the doctor's surgery or library, the decorative case of the town-hall clock, a display in a shop window or a pub sign. The point here is that we all see and notice differently – we each have our personal history of looking, which means we'll be drawn to different objects, colours or textures. This is particularly useful when it comes to looking at contemporary art or sculpture because, as you know, it tends to provoke quite strong reaction when it 'invades' the public realm. People often resent changes to familiar views, especially if the sculpture, the invading object, is something that is not easily and quickly understood, for example an abstract piece. So walking together, talking about what you see together and giving art the time to make itself clear to you will broaden the vision and give you a wider repertoire to choose from. If you do have some contemporary art work in the locality, you might be able to contact the artist and invite them to come and speak to you or the school about the work from their perspective.

Your team walk could usefully be complemented by one with the children. As with all learning outside the classroom, you will find out more about what interests them and what motivates their personal learning, and they are likely to show you something you have never noticed! As I observed when I visited Cleveland Road Primary School, among several others, when children contribute to their own curriculum, they have many reasons to have a committed buy-in to it.

Having found a number of unique pieces in your neighbourhood that you feel are worth spending time with, it will then be up to you and your team to work out how they might fit with and animate your curriculum. One possibility would be to photograph what you find, perhaps choosing interesting viewpoints (a statue from low down to draw attention to its size, the profile view of a building feature to emphasise a relief or a close-up of a small detail). The images could be printed and mounted together to make a composite. If it's a successful piece, celebrate it with an exhibition in school or find a local exhibiting opportunity for it. All this could fit into the context of a local history or geography unit or take you in other inventive directions, and maybe it will also lead to interesting and fruitful community connections.

Perhaps you feel that there isn't anyone on your staff who could manage the art element of such a project. One of the schools I visited had done a really productive audit of teachers, governors and other staff, and also of school families and community contacts, to see whether they had any expertise that the head felt would benefit the school. There may be a TA, a parent or grandparent with a secret passion for, say, photography, who could either work alongside class teachers, focusing on skills, or do a specialist INSET for them. Or, if you can find the budget, it may be possible to buy in an artist-educator to deliver it. We'll look at examples of this later in this chapter on page 34.

Looking closely: visiting art spaces

When we can use the free art resources of the neighbouring world outside the school, what might the benefits be of making a trip to an art gallery or museum, particularly when this may involve teachers in more risk assessments and forms than they feel they need, as well as costly, sometimes lengthy travel and, perhaps most crucially for many schools, up to a whole precious day off-curriculum?

Many galleries are reporting a reduced uptake of their learning and education services. A 2017 report by the Department for Culture, Media and Sport (DCMS) showed a 6.9 per cent decrease (after adjustment) in educational visits and participation in on-site activities for under-18s in DCMS-supported museums and galleries (Jones, 2017). Anecdotally, teachers quote precisely the reasons listed above to account for their own reluctance to make such visits.

Nevertheless the services are still there. Some are even still free to local schools and here are my arguments for carrying on making the visits, or starting to do so if such visits don't happen much in your school.

Firstly and most fundamentally, as *Guardian* art critic Jonathan Jones (2017) says, 'There is nothing more aspirational than visiting a museum or art gallery. It is an expression of hope and self-esteem.' When most of our big public museums and galleries were built in the 19th century, they were funded by philanthropists who wanted to provide enlightenment and pleasure for a wide public. One of the founding principles of the National Gallery, London was to locate in an area that was as near to the poor East End as to the richer West End. Admission to it was to be free and, unusually for the 1830s, children were allowed in, partly to ensure that mothers who didn't have nursemaids could also visit. When I work with children in these kinds of spaces they say things like, 'This is the most beautiful place I've ever been to.' A visit to a gallery or museum can offer a unique opening of mind and eyes to new ideas and new expressive takes on the world; as records of human artistic achievement and holders of meaning, museums can inspire optimism, as Jones says, as well as sparking creative ambition.

If you need more convincing than that, museums and galleries bring to vivid life core curriculum areas such as history (through encounters with authentic objects or paintings from past periods), English (as we'll see, artworks can be wonderful jumping-off points for creative or factual writing) and art itself (where techniques and subjects can serve as models and stimuli). Learning staff are usually available to help you to tailor such a themed visit if you feel you can't justify a generic visit to a gallery for its own sake. Many galleries offer creative sessions where artist-teachers work, usually with relatively small groups, and make art in response to the gallery collection. These have costs attached and are often one-off events. My feelings about this way of outsourcing subject teaching is that in my ideal school the artists would be there in classrooms (something Grafton Primary School, London, has done for example; see page 34), and, even more perfectly, they may even be class teachers too. Either way, they can be there embedding the learning they have to offer throughout the school, as well as being able to accompany children on gallery visits.

So how might a really impactful gallery visit work? The children and accompanying adults should be prepared for the experience, in the sense that they know what kind of place they are visiting (I once had a child ask me at the door of the National Gallery whether they were visiting a zoo…). They should not be over-prepared though, especially if you are using the services of learning staff; something fairly generic about the place and its collections and what sort of behaviour would be expected is enough. We know that being surprised is also a pleasurable part of the whole experience.

After that, I would always keep in mind a sense of 'less is more' and not recommend a visit of more than two hours including lunch. If you have a session led by an educator they will probably only look at a few objects – maybe three or four in an hour. When, as part of the education team at the National Gallery, I used to discuss prospective visits with teachers, they would often ask how many works they would see, and would sometimes question my answer. Surely, they would argue, it was a wasted opportunity for their class to make a long journey to a well-known gallery and not see all the highlight works. But if you have ever been to a big blockbuster exhibition and tried to remember what you saw, or anything much about your responses, you'll know that it's impossible either to do any of the works proper justice, or to retain useful information. When writing their post-visit evaluations, teachers rarely commented on not seeing enough and almost always understood and appreciated that focusing on a few objects very intensively had led to children's excellent recall of the session. I once had to spend time in Newark station cafe waiting for a delayed train. The cafe was very quiet and the young woman behind the counter asked what I was doing in Newark. I explained I was from the National Gallery and had been to visit a primary school for the Take One Picture scheme. When I mentioned the Gallery the woman's eyes lit up: 'The National Gallery?' she said. 'We went there on a school trip ages ago and I really remember one of the pictures.' She went on to describe Titian's *Bacchus and Ariadne* (Illustration 2.5) – not the artist's name or the title, but instead, and in great and loving detail, the colour of the sky, what the people were wearing and how they were posed. She remembered in particular a man who, she said, excitedly, was 'holding a leg of lamb above his head, like this!' and reaching into the cold counter in front of her, she took out a ham on the bone and swung it about her own head, with delight. As you can imagine, this was a rewarding moment for an educator. So, less is more: there is a disease called museum fatigue; it's a very pernicious one and has been known to put people off for life...

In the gallery I have only one other piece of advice, which is another of the key strands in the book: to listen to children. In the USA, museum education is often carried out by volunteers known as docents. Without in any way caricaturing them, I'll characterise them as well-meaning, mainly comfortably-off women of a certain age, who have memorised a script about a set number of exhibits. When a child comments on or asks a question about a work on the wall that is not in this script, the docent is often unable to respond. Then a good learning opportunity has vanished, and a child may have been disappointed or thinks they've asked a bad question.

So when I work with children in an art setting, while having in mind approaches and information that I would want them to know by the end of the session, I always start with their first responses. As an example, here's a little dialogue I recorded with some Year 3 children. We went to the National Gallery and I decided to let them choose the first image themselves (we would then see others relevant to their topic).

Walking into a large room crowded with many pictures, two children were immediately drawn to a large baroque work by the 17th-century Neapolitan artist, Luca Giordano (see Illustration 2.6). Titled *Perseus Turning Phineas and His Followers to Stone*, it shows a dramatic moment in the story of the Ancient Greek hero Perseus. He has returned from his mission to cut off the monster Medusa's snake-haired head, where he needed to look at her face in his shield in order to stop her from turning him to stone. On his way home he rescues the princess Andromeda from the grasp of another monster, on condition that she marries him. The painting shows the wedding feast of Perseus and Andromeda at the moment when Phineas, her previous boyfriend, arrives with his henchmen to reclaim her and punish Perseus. Averting his eyes from it himself, Perseus thrusts Medusa's head towards his three adversaries, who are in the process of being turned to stone. When you spend time looking, you notice that the image actually depicts a stage performance of the story, with the background being a painted backdrop, the dark spaces of the wings visible on both sides, and the light from a spot streaming towards Perseus.

GK:	Why did you choose this picture to look at?
Child A:	Because of the chopped-off head, because someone was holding a head, and they're having a fight.
GK:	Yes! It's a picture of a story. What kind of story might it be?
Child B:	A story about an angry mob!
Child C:	Or a hero story?
GK:	Yes, I wonder which kind of hero story? What's the hero wearing?
Child A:	Armour and funny boots with nothing covering the toes.
GK:	Any other clues about the story that this hero is in? What about the head?
Child D:	It's very dark and grey.
Child F:	And it has snake hair! I've seen the movie and I've heard about it but I can't remember its name… when it looks at people they turn into stone.
GK:	Yes, it's the story of Perseus from the Greek myths.
Child D:	Oh yes, the Greek myths!
GK:	And he was a hero whose mission was to destroy the monster Medusa. This was hard if he couldn't look at her without turning into stone. How do you think he managed it?
Child G:	Don't know. Tell us!
GK:	He used his shield as a mirror and then he could see where she was.
Child B:	That's like Harry Potter and the basilisk!
GK:	And now he was on his way home when on the way he saw the princess Andromeda, who was being threatened by a terrible sea monster. He said he'd rescue her on condition that she married him. What do you think her answer was?
Child H:	Yes!
GK:	It was and this is a picture of their wedding feast.
Child A:	It doesn't look like a wedding…
GK:	Not very but can you see any clues that it was?
Child J:	There are lots of plates stacked up, jars of wine…
Child K:	And a tablecloth.
Child C:	But why is there a wall and a door? It looks like a city?
Child D:	Perhaps it's an outside wedding…

Visual and plastic arts

GK:	We'll come back to that in a minute. Let's finish the story… So the three men rushing in from the left are Andromeda's boyfriend and his mates. He is very angry and is trying to attack Perseus. What could he do to defend himself?
Child A:	Fight back, use his sword?
Child K:	No, he uses the head to turn them to stone!
Child C:	And look, one of the men is half turning to stone! He's a bit dark…
GK:	You've got it.
Child B:	But why is Perseus looking the other way? They'd be able to kill him.
GK:	Good question. What do you think?
Child C:	There's no action where he's looking.
Child G:	Maybe he doesn't really care about them.
Child A:	No, he doesn't want to look at the head. He's looking away from the head so that he doesn't get turned into stone by it and they do!
GK:	Yes! Now let's go back to the wall and the city – what can you see to the left and the right of it?
Child K:	Dark bits.
GK:	Yes, and can you see where the light is coming from?
Child A:	Yes, it's streaming down onto Perseus.
GK:	What kind of place has dark bits on the side and light coming in from one direction?
Child A:	A dark room with a window?
Child J:	A cinema?
Child B:	No, a theatre!
GK:	Yes, a theatre! This picture is of a play of the story of Perseus and they're on a stage.
Child D:	And so it's a fake head!
Child A:	It must have been a very experienced painter who painted it…

The many exclamation marks are the best indication I can give of the excitement in these children's voices, as the meaning of the picture gradually unfolded in front of them, almost like a performance. I was questioning them in a leading way, although accepting all answers as possibilities, but the best moment for me was when Child B began interrogating the picture himself: 'But why is Perseus looking the other way? They'd be able to kill him.' He had picked up on the cue the artist has given us that Perseus must look the other way to prevent himself being turned to stone, applied his own logic that you wouldn't look the other way if you were being attacked, and needed to know the answer. Proper active learning.

This process is all about starting with the child and the art object. When you adopt an approach that is about open-ended enquiry, children will all learn something by trying to answer the question together, and having realised that you can ask questions about a work, they start to do the same thing. You'll have noticed that the artist's name didn't figure in that conversation, nor their biography nor any dates. This discussion is much more about the learning process – about how you look at and interrogate a work, apply reasoning and try to understand it. And about the reward that you get when you do work something out for yourself. Some of the knowledge comes that way and further information can easily be researched online later.

The other element of the discussion was the personal response – the right not to like something is paramount, even if the work belongs to a respected canon. People's responses to art often reveal their own story in quite a deep way, and if someone has a negative reaction to a work by Van Gogh that I really like, they must have their own good reasons. It would be our job to find out why, to develop critical vocabulary and perhaps learn something about our own personal taste.

I was once working with a group of 15-year-old Bangladeshi girls from a school in East London. They were doing GCSE art and we looked at Velazquez's *Christ in the House of Martha and Mary* (see Illustration 2.7). The picture is a rich and many-layered one, which I often used with primary children if they were doing a food or cookery topic. The food in this image is lusciously painted and I've had some wonderful recipe suggestions for the ingredients spread out on the table, in a MasterChef-like way, including fish curry with a hard-boiled egg on top. But these girls were also interested in both the figure of the girl, who looks out at us with such a pleadingly sad expression, and the little scene taking place in the window-like opening on the right. It actually represents Jesus visiting the house of two of his friends, sisters Martha and Mary. Mary sits on the floor listening to him speaking but Martha feels stuck in the kitchen and remonstrates about this. I didn't tell the girls this story but was encouraging them to construct some kind of meaning using the evidence in the picture. A girl who had been sitting silently at the back for most of the hour suddenly put up her hand. 'I know what it means,' she said. 'That window is actually a mirror and so the girl in the front is looking at the people who are actually in front of her, and they are arranging a marriage for her. That's why she's sad. It makes me sad.'

Such a raw and authentic response is one of the reasons why a rich arts education is so important. This young woman was making sense of a situation in her life or that of someone close to her (the fact that a marriage might be arranged against her will) through a work of 17th-century Spanish art – culturally speaking, a world away in time and geography from her. Its highly skilled execution and emotional truthfulness was able to communicate with her across the centuries.

But what about more contemporary art? Many teachers I speak with say they don't know how to approach it or feel uncertain about talking about it: perhaps this is about the norm for them being work that is figurative and representational, work that is relatively easy to take in at a glance. My answer would be to look at it in the same enquiring way as that described above. The work may look simple – take this sculpture (Illustration 2.8, *Incommunicado*) by the Palestinian artist Mona Hatoum, from the Tate collection. At first sight it's an everyday object – a baby's cot. But then the question has to be: what is it doing in an art gallery? It's our job to find an answer. So, look more closely, see that it's probably not a cot we would want to put our child in. A cot should stand for care and protection, but this one is made of cold, hard steel and there's no soft padding. It's too small for a comfortable sleep, and, worst of all, the base is actually constructed of vicious cheese wire, stretched taut. A place of rest has turned into a harsh, torturing prison. This provokes the next question: why would an artist do that? And that in turn raises the additional question about whether art is always 'beautiful' or easy on the eye. Some of Hatoum's work alludes to her experience of exile: firstly when her parents were forced to leave their homeland for Beirut during the Arab-Israeli conflict, and later when she found herself stranded in London when the Lebanese Civil War broke out. She decided to stay in London and attended art school.

I can guarantee that you could take a Year 6 class to see this work and leave the gallery having had a serious and important discussion about metaphor (the cot as prison, then the state as parent who tortures their own child), and about the medium of expression. As a result, back in school a conceptual sculpture could be made about refugees and exile, or a more factual 2D image could be created to communicate the same message. Children will probably raise other linked themes themselves. I would show this to children in connection with a history unit on war, for example, because it would engage them imaginatively and empathetically with the subject – yet another outcome of an arts-rich curriculum. Heads often say that they find that non-specialist teachers feel challenged by the 3D art element of the curriculum, but the idea of altering an everyday object to represent feelings about an issue or an experience is an activity that they may feel is more within their reach.

Some galleries have extensive learning or education departments who will be able to help you create the visit you would like. There are exciting collaborative initiatives in which galleries such as The Hepworth Wakefield are really trying to work with schools in order to be able to maximise their offers to them. Their 'Join the Conversation' events ensure that the arguments for an arts-rich curriculum can be properly aired with teachers and specialist speakers. The National Gallery is still running Take One Picture, now involving many more schools; there is a vast archive of truly creative responses to the Gallery's collection of paintings. The Whitworth Gallery in Manchester offers pioneering initiatives involving masterclasses with mathematicians and musicians making cross-disciplinary links with art, and most public galleries offer practical artist-led sessions as well as self-guiding opportunities.

Whatever kind of public gallery is available to you – it absolutely doesn't have to be a big National – it will be an asset worth exploiting. If it's a small, local gallery, you may need to ask to partner up with their staff and co-create a programme that suits you both. Whichever route you take, galleries are spaces of unexpected encounters with what artists of the past and present have to say, of works you can easily link with many curriculum areas, and of techniques children will want to try out for themselves. They are places that ideally they will later want to return to with their families.

The school as art gallery: 'All Schools Should Be Art Schools'

'All Schools Should Be Art Schools' are words on a 2017 artwork by Bob and Roberta Smith (this is the pseudonym for the contemporary British artist, Patrick Brill). It was created as part of Yorkshire Sculpture Park's 40th anniversary celebrations. It's a large-scale, colourful painted graphic work of the above words, which express the artist Bob and Roberta Smith's concern with the diminishing role of the arts in schools. As in his other painted works, it's an example of an artist's aim to appeal for political action and forms a part of his campaign for improved arts education. Seeing this inspirational work at the Yorkshire Sculpture Park last year reminded me of something I had come across in Paris a couple of years earlier.

I had been wandering in galleries and found a little exhibition at the Musée du Petit Palais. It was called 'L'École joyeuse et parée' (roughly translated as 'the happy, decorated school') and on display were designs and finished works that had been produced to adorn the walls of Paris state primary schools between about 1880 and 1940. The exhibition title came from an official bulletin of the 1930s, where the vice-president of the Paris town council was describing a new concept for primary education, which had been free and mandatory for all children since 1881:

> 'in former days the school [building] was an airless and charmless place: bare earth, the [whipping] bogeyman, punishment, it was face to the wall, again and again… It was the school as prison and then the school as factory… now we want the happy, decorated school' (Riotor, in Collet and Monfort, 2013, my own translation)

To achieve this, the good education officers of the time invested in many new schools and invited artists to propose schemes for large murals to cover the walls of these new buildings. It was felt that not only would children benefit from the improved environment that these images would create, but also that they would be motivational tools for learning:

> 'children must live surrounded by… works that speak to their eyes… awaken their curiosity and raise up their souls' (Bigot, in Collet and Monfort, 2013, my own translation)

The subjects of these works varied: there were pictures of famous French cities, scenes from history and illustrations to well-known books of the time such as La Fontaine's *Fables*. The four seasons were represented, as well as landscapes and people working or at play. Some were definitely intended to be morally improving, others more freely imaginative. The images were either painted or made in mosaic and they were all of very high quality. There was a feeling of lightness and optimism in these rooms, of children being respected and encouraged through art, and I left dreaming of artists I would want to invite to produce similar contemporary schemes in our schools today.

As it happened, a couple of years later I found out that the Hepworth Gallery in Wakefield had announced plans to re-launch a pioneering scheme from the late 1940s known as the 'School Prints' series, which in some ways echoed the aims of the Paris venture. Brenda Rawnsley, who was later to be married to the art education guru Herbert Read, developed an idea her late husband Derek had had of commissioning recognised British artists to make original lithographs (prints) for loaning to schools. Brenda decided to grow the scheme by making very large editions of the prints, which would be then be sold at a reasonable price to schools, who would in turn commit to the scheme by subscribing to three annual sets. The pedagogical aim was for children in schools to have real works of art around them. In her introductory letter to artists, Brenda Rawnsley wrote, 'We are producing a series of auto-lithographs, four for each term, for use in schools, as a means of giving school children an understanding of contemporary art.' (Rawnsley in Artmonsky, 2006). The artists for the two earlier series included names such as L.S. Lowry, John Nash and Feliks Topolski.

Following some success with these, Rawnsley then became ambitious for the art to be more international. In 1947 she bravely commissioned works by the best-known contemporary artists in France: Georges Braque, Pablo Picasso, Fernand Léger and Henri Matisse, little realising what opposition such 'modern' works would provoke, both in the press and from her clients, the schools. The Picasso, a lively and brightly coloured work in Cubist style, drew particular vitriol. The *Evening Standard* said on 10 May 1949:

> '*Of the educationalists who have visited the exhibition at School Prints Studio, one said it was a bird drinking, a second said it was Picasso himself lying in a hammock, a third said a woman in an aeroplane. Picasso refuses to explain the drawing and says, "The children will understand."*' (sic, The Evening Standard *in Artmonsky, 2006)*

This was intended to be a fairly typical press put-down of modern art, but for all of that it also makes one good point in favour of the work (although the British teachers of the 1940s cancelled their subscriptions to the scheme in large numbers when they saw the artworks and it was the end of the scheme). Picasso was right; children do naturally 'understand' complex images, or at least they give them their best chance. The Hepworth Gallery have picked up on this in their 2018 re-launch of the scheme, and their first series of School Prints has been launched with the work of six British artists: Martin Creed, Jeremy Deller, Anthea Hamilton,

Helen Marten, Haroon Mirza and Rose Wylie. The works are bold and as challenging as the 1949 set, but what seems to have helped with the new version is that the Hepworth has a deep engagement with the six local schools that are trialling the scheme. So there is a level of trust between gallery and teachers that seems to have reassured any initial doubters.

We may not have the school budgets to buy original artworks such as the Schools Prints, and perhaps our approach to decoration today would be less paternalistic than the 1930s Paris scheme, but I did recently visit a school that had managed to create a similar transformative effect with art, though by very different means.

Case study 1: Grafton Primary School, Islington, London

When I first opened the door to the reception area of Grafton School, a large red-brick Victorian building just off North London's bustling Holloway Road, I felt a bit of a 'soul lift' myself. My eyes were drawn upwards, where a huge, airy, multicoloured sculpture was suspended, twisting and winding its way across the whole space. When you have visited as many different primary schools as I have, it's not hard to nose out the school ethos pretty quickly: its visual appearance gives many things away. Here it was very evident that this large artwork made by children working with an artist-teacher embodies the school's vision for creative learning: it is an upfront statement to visitors of the value this school places on a stimulating and beautiful learning environment for children, staff and visitors. It speaks of the spaces carved out in the curriculum for all the children to learn arts skills and create works of art themselves. This vision welcomed you like a warm smile into that reception space and it was there from floor to ceiling in every corridor and every classroom from Reception to Year 6.

Why and how was this achieved? I asked the head Nitsa Sergides and deputy Anna Sutton about their reasons for taking this particular pedagogical route:

NS: *I love coming into Grafton. Every day I'm personally inspired by the beautiful displays – I look at that art work and every day it tells me a different story. I would say that you've got to understand the importance of the creative arts in a child's life, and what children really need to do when they're in primary school – and you yourself have to appreciate the creative arts properly if they're going to make a difference to the child. Of course reading and writing and maths are crucially important subjects… in the emotional, social and cognitive sense, everything. However if you don't have the creative arts to colour children's days then how poor are they? As a result of our strong arts curriculum, a real feature of our school is our behaviour – I've not excluded a child for 15 years. If you walk into the classrooms they'll be getting on with their work. They've got a beautiful environment – an aesthetically pleasing place.*

AS: *Some of our children don't have very rich environments in their homes so they love to come in here. And they buy into it; they look after the displays. And because of our curriculum our results have gone up and up. When Nitsa and I were first here it was a sink school. It was a hard place to work in and we couldn't fill a year group… but a year ago we were in the top ten schools in London and top two per cent in the country.*

NS: *We believe strongly that you are the person who is going to decide what is the priority for your children. It's a bit like putting food on a table for them – you choose between what's healthy and what isn't. We do make sure that we balance what we give them and we would never let the arts go.*

As for how Grafton goes on developing their vision and making it happen, one of the answers is by recruiting a wide group of specialist resident arts teachers to complement the work of class teachers. You do of course take a risk when you employ artist teachers: artists are usually people with personal ambitions and visions, who are sometimes less good as team players. At Grafton, though, they have brought together art, music, dance, drama and creative writing professionals who are also trained teachers and who see supporting and training class teachers as an important element of their role.

In the staffroom at Grafton, I spoke with Tessa Garland, responsible for the sculpture in reception and most of the rest of the school displays. Here's what she said.

My story
I'm an artist and I've got my own practice and it's my key thing, but early on in my career as an artist it was very hard to earn money and I've always enjoyed working in education – in teaching. I started to work in a theatre group called Knee High Theatre in Cornwall many years ago and it was such a good experience. We had no training and it was more like skills-based sharing: we learned skills, which we then taught to school groups. I remember my first teaching session was actually terrible. We were making structures – I actually came from sculpture so I've got those 3D making skills and I should have known better. But bit by bit I learned to teach and then later on, always keeping my practice, I moved from sculpture into installation and video but I still draw. Then I thought I should teach full time so I did a primary PGCE. I soon realised I didn't want to become a teacher but I enjoyed teaching. So what I do now is a solution to that problem. When I started working as an artist in primary schools, it was at a time when heads had a pot of money for an arts week so I would devise a project and there would be an outcome. At the same time in Cornwall I worked on quite a few festivals where the collaboration was brilliant. I worked with writers and poets and painters and theatre people and I picked up many skills that I still have. I moved to London and one of my first artist-educator jobs was working on a Creative Partnerships project with Grafton. I came here in 2003, met Nitsa, looked around and thought this is different; there's a lot of art here and it's a good environment. I felt at home. I was offered a job here (three days a week, as I didn't want to lose my practice) and I've done it ever since.

In the classroom
I work across the school, Year 1 through to Year 6, and I have half a term per year group and that seems to work out. I have three contact days and I'm flexible in the school [as we were speaking, a teacher came into the staffroom and said: 'I'm going to need some of your expertise, Tessa. We're doing an assembly

on teeth!']. *Because of my theatre experience I make props I slot into the shows* – *end of year leavers' assembly and things like that. They'll give me the script and we'll meet, work out what we need and make costumes. We work from the art hut and children come and go, and I'm easy with that.*

I also go into classes and my work there is to teach art skills, and we'll end up with a finished piece. So for example I did the Take One Picture's scheme picture one term, which was Renoir's Umbrellas. I presented the painting, we worked with sketchbooks and then I took four groups of eight children for a quarter of the day to make something bigger.

We also do schemes that are less skills-based, for example we do the Fourth Plinth Schools Awards [where school-age children suggest ideas for sculpture to be placed on the empty Fourth Plinth in Trafalgar Square]. *I like it because I'm also very open to kids' ideas.*

I introduce the scheme and give it context; I then give each child a sheet of paper and they take it away for two weeks and make a drawing or model. Next they present these in the hall and on the website. It's always different children and it's basically ideas focused rather than skills based. This is a really different area for me. One little girl came up with a Barbie doll – I thought, I'm not sure about this, but she said, 'No, it's not *a Barbie doll because I've cut off her hair and reclothed her...', and there was some work by another girl who made this beautiful cut-out. She never spoke but she had this amazing imagination.*

I also run a scheme with my classes called 'artist of the month'. I'll talk to the teacher and we'll select a child (usually one who needs a boost in confidence) and I give them a canvas and brushes and the child makes their own painting and we present them at the whole-school assembly.

There's a lot of excitement and love and struggle, and confidence. When I first go into a class it's about getting children to be confident and about being in the engagement zone. I try to point that out to them – I'll say, 'Is that a good place to be?', and they say yes! You've got to get the environment right and lead children to that place. It's often peaceful; you find a deep level of concentration. I think it's a little bit about tapping into the self and finding a language, and then pointing out that everyone's drawing is different. There's no right or wrong; it's about difference and celebrating that in a non-competitive way. But of course when I teach I'm also very structured – it's always stage by stage.

We're very experimental here. My experience of being freelance is useful because it gives me lots of ideas: we've got a paper rolling machine to make sculptures, we've done frescoes using modroc or plaster where we've done drawings onto the plaster, we've done digital projects, where children took photos of each other and manipulated them and then worked with their photographs. I find that, overall, children who struggle with drawing skills are often good at textures or other ways of expressing themselves.

Working with teachers

Class teachers do teach art in their classes too. They're good at picking up skills and when I'm teaching art I want them to be hands-on with me, and present, and they always are, so they get involved. And they know their children. I think it's reassuring for them to have someone confident around who knows their stuff. From me they might learn about drawing a face, a portrait – some are quite ambitious. People often come down to me in the art room with queries and I try to give them a bit of time to help them out. We also work together on projects – the leavers' assembly, some projects with the writer-in-residence or animations. For Take One Picture we made a soundtrack with the music teacher for example. All the creatives always come together for World Day and that's very collaborative. You have to be free flowing at this school and willing to change your plans and be adaptable!

Display

The work you can see here on the walls, some of it goes back a long way and it's quite unique. Nitsa wants to keep everything – the teenagers come back and see work they made years before. I've made so much work in the school that some of it needs a bit of maintenance now and I've been given a bit of time to go round making good. I look at the old and new stuff and I see it makes a really engaging learning environment. There's so much to see all the time. We decorated the IT room, for example, so it's full of high-tech equipment and low-tech art. Every time I put up something new it's always interesting to stand around and listen. Children and staff will always look and make comments... we're running out of space now though. I do put lots of effort into presentation – I'm not a carpenter but I made frames for some mosaics we did, and I'm also not a mosaicist but I learned on YouTube!

The art hut

[A wooden structure at the far end of the playground. It is reached through a wild garden, where children do science investigations.]

This is a working studio. It's mainly my space but there's a parents club and arts club that use it too. It's a bit basic but this is what it is. This is our toilet, the most beautiful toilet in the world! [The walls are decorated with all kinds of art.] *These are props for the Year 6 leaving assembly – it's like a graveyard of old props. Sometimes we reuse things – that tree from the leavers' assembly keeps being reused for example. I hold all my materials here; some are shared materials but I keep track of all the stuff – I have to – I have an art budget but it's much less since teachers' wages went up!*

The school

Having been at Grafton a while I can see that although governments and education ministers have come and gone, the school has always had the same ethos. They're very rigorous here and everyone is really hard-working, but Nitsa recognises the importance of creativity and she knows that children get improved self-esteem through it, which helps raise attainment and motivation. They're happy kids and I'm pretty happy arriving every day!

Tessa is only one of many talented arts professionals working at Grafton School. Her testimony demonstrates some of the advantages a school can derive from employing people like her: as an artist she has a rich and diverse work experience, so she brings new ideas, new approaches and ways of working from the world outside; she has her own practice, so her own creativity is still being stimulated; she is thinking like an artist; she also has

> deep knowledge of how art materials work, of how to find good-quality resources cheaply, and of how to look after paintbrushes properly; to children she offers a model of a creative professional's life as something to aspire to; she is an artist who is also a trained teacher, so she understands the job of class teaching and is flexible enough to be able to co-operate with and support non-specialist staff. In turn, the school community has understood the value she brings to them: the CPD for class teachers, the collaboration with colleagues and the large 3D displays that so characterise the appearance of the school. More than decorations, these are objects that are loved by children, staff and visitors; they are the school's collective memory, representing moments of pleasure, learning and achievement through skilled, concentrated work. No wonder then that, like the art we may have on our walls at home, which forms part of our domestic landscape, the Grafton family want to keep many of them as significant and meaningful features of theirs.

So make the most of visual art!

The visual arts, being non-verbal, are, along with dance and music, the most accessible of the art forms, both in the making and in the understanding of them: they allow every child to succeed at their own level. A child might need good fine motor skills for observational drawing but, as Tessa pointed out, if they don't have these, they may instead excel in making textures, or have a great eye with the camera, or a highly developed sense of colour, or ideas for more conceptual art like the girl with the Barbie doll. From time to time I have led gallery sessions with groups of children from the traveller community. These children, who sometimes have very poor levels of literacy, were exceptionally adept at looking at art and constructing credible and logical meaning around it.

Developing visual literacy through good and early engagement with picture book art, through large and prominent displays of children's art and reproductions of work by professional artists (which promotes critical discussion), and through visiting art spaces such as galleries and museums, is something you can easily integrate. If you feel that there is no one in your current team who has really grasped the art of good display, schools like Grafton and others in this book are always happy to share their knowledge and experience.

When it comes to making art, which the National Curriculum does of course require, if none of your teaching staff have confident skills, then your audit of the wider community may well turn up someone who does. Barcombe Primary School in Sussex found that they had a teaching assistant, Penny Edwards, who was enthusiastic and skilled enough to take on the lead art role in their village school. Not only did she ensure that the art curriculum was delivered in a way that did proper justice to it in terms of time, resources and display, but she also extended her remit to the outdoor spaces, creating a story garden (gardeners who create beautiful gardens also count as artists in my eyes; think about the aesthetic decisions they make – colours and textures that sing together, creating pleasing views for the eye to explore). This garden was set in a sympathetically designed space looking out over an inspiring rural landscape, and Penny also used the extensive school grounds for family activities. In connection with a project around Quentin Blake's *Angel Pavement*, a picture book about a pavement artist, she held a family drawing day in the playground, where families were given a packet of chalks and spent time free drawing on the unrestricted expanse of tarmac. This activity transformed the space, which is always a good artistic principle because art helps people see differently. It also gave an opportunity for adults to connect with their own creativity, which as we've noticed has so often been suppressed, and was a really successful example of intergenerational learning.

This chapter is an invitation to make your school a visual school. The connection between looking at art and making it is a close and dynamic one; yes, you may need your working walls for maths and English, but it's the imagery, the generous amount of it, the range of its media and expression, that's really going to inspire the whole community of your school.

Chapter 3
Music

> *'Learning music is a birthright. And you have to start young.'*
> (Sir Simon Rattle, 2014)

Of all the arts, the teaching of music is perhaps the one that causes most anxiety among non-specialist teachers. Instrumental skills can seem magically unattainable to those who don't have them, many teachers don't trust their singing voices and, as for composition, if you don't have the grammar of music behind you it can feel like a big challenge. But before talking about the compensatory role that music specialists can play, let's look at what is easily possible in a classroom and why it's important.

Start with rhythm

Before each of us was born, we were already in a sound world coloured by rhythm of one kind or another: our mother's heartbeat, the rhythm of her walking or running, the pulses of her speech. So it's not surprising that babies as young as six months old have been shown to respond to musical pulse by moving to it, more or less in rhythm. If you are a parent or have experience of very young children, you'll have seen the delighted way a baby shakes her head or waves her hands to music with a good beat. So there is also a connection between external rhythm and physical movement, which you know because you've been in a club or stadium or other music venue and felt irresistibly driven to join in the music on stage with your own body.

Scientists such as Dr Nina Kraus and Dr Laurel Trainor have demonstrated how the brain is programmed to pick up on natural rhythmic patterns – but more than that, how children who have been exposed to music of all kinds through participatory activities from a young age have enhanced language skills; how in children with autism, rhythm work has been shown to help them to organise their sometimes confused sensory world (see The Kennedy Center, 2018). You only have to watch the historic video of the pioneering music therapists Nordoff and Robbins working with children with profound communication disabilities to see how musical rhythms can help these (and all) children make good human connections with others. You can find it here: https://www.nordoff-robbins.org.uk/what-is-music-therapy.

So beating or clapping a rhythm is a most basic and enjoyable form of music making. It sometimes seems to me that teachers give a slightly mixed message about this invigorating, pleasurable activity when they use it as a method of silencing a noisy class, with the children clapping the same rhythm back. Making children connect performing rhythm with a feeling of being brought into line may not be the best way of creating positive associations with it.

However, creating activities around rhythm is within everyone's reach, and even non-specialist teachers who might be afraid of singing can address some of the curriculum requirements *and* create an upbeat approach to the day's work by occasionally starting a day with five minutes of rhythm activity. Reading a rhythmic poem would definitely count, and so would something like teacher Andrea Pyne's 'Don't clap this one back' (a version of Simon Says). In this activity, a teacher claps a short rhythm using hands together or hands on other parts of the body or the floor. If the children hear the rhythm of 'don't clap this one back' they must not clap it back. When a child does clap the rhythm the teacher gets a point, but if no one does then it's the children who get the point.

Rhythm is also a concept that, like many elements in all the arts subjects, has unexpected echoes in several curriculum areas. Imagine doing a whole-school focus on rhythm: it works in PE (gymnastics) and of course in both dance and music, where you could work with drums or other untuned percussion; in maths or visual arts it might translate as repeating pattern; in English it could be metre in poetry or the rhythms of speech; in science it may be the seasons as rhythms of nature, or the rhythm of bird wings in flight or insects at work; in physics it could include the pattern of sound waves. Teachers will find so many more ways of exploring it creatively. Whichever way you go, it could all add up to a grand foot-tapping sharing assembly or, more ambitiously, as the theme for the end-of-term school show.

Rhythm, then, is one of music's most basic and necessary elements. In the National Curriculum for music it's described as 'duration' and the other dimensions of music are listed as pitch, dynamics, tempo, timbre, texture, structure and notations. But rhythm is the only one that exists within us as human beings. We literally breathe it all day and night; it's the heartbeat, the one we all get straight away. Rhythm is elemental and powerful, can galvanise or quieten and we should pay it the attention it deserves.

Sing more!

'Around the world, caregivers sing to infants in a way that differs from most other kinds of singing – usually in a conversational style, with a lot of repetition, high in pitch, slow in tempo, and in a loving tone of voice. Infants prefer this over other styles of singing.' (Trainor, 2013)

Just as we know that rhythm is a vital early part of our auditory world, we also know that as babies the first pitched sounds we usually hear are from a parent, most often a mother, singing and that such singing really does have an effect on the baby. Laurel Trainor (2013) has shown how parents and carers use singing to help control a child's state: either to soothe distress, to quieten or to animate and amuse. Trainor suggests that singing keeps infants calm twice as long as any other kind of intervention. As adults, we all know how the sung music we heard as teenagers seemed to reflect our condition – not only the lyrics about love and loss and being an outsider, but the combination of these with a strong, memorable tune. So there's a connection between listening to singing and our emotional state.

But what about doing it? How does singing contribute to the life of a successful school? Richard Frostick is a dynamic former teacher, adviser and Ofsted inspector, who, among many other of his projects, founded and continues to run Music Centre London (MCL). This is a weekend centre, which currently functions in the London boroughs of Southwark and Islington, and the Centre recruits its children from local state primary schools. At the beginning of the academic year, Richard or one of his small team tours the schools in each borough, dropping off application forms in the school offices: he now knows both heads and office staff, which he sees as a vital part of the trusting relationship that is the basis of this kind of partnership. MCL is one of the now numerous organisations that have been created to improve music education for children of school age, and it exists to address a shortfall in the provision of music in primary schools. We don't need to rehearse the reasons for this shortfall, but, to be positive, let's say that the work that goes on at the MCL – choral and instrumental tuition – is the kind of teaching that is in fact still taking place in some schools, as we'll see in the case study on page 55.

Commenting on one of the recent notable by-products of the programme (one that he was not actually considering when he planned the MCL 25 years ago), Richard told me:

> 'At the music centre a number of parents were concerned that their children were showing signs of real stress – mainly those doing Key Stage 2 SATs in the run-up to the May date. One mother said her son had started bedwetting again after four or five years; others were describing their children as irritable or sullen. A lot of these parents told me it was so good for their children to come along on a Saturday and just sing, where there was no pressure on them to deliver any measurable outcome, where they could just be children, and have fun with music, be expressive.'

So 'just singing' and 'having fun' is a start.

On this matter, Richard leads many singing CPD programmes for teachers, both in the UK and internationally. He is currently artistic director of a groundbreaking singing education project funded by the British Council called World Voice. His description of the way these sessions often develop is instructive. He explained to me:

> 'I get teachers to find the creativity in themselves – it's complicated but also very simple. I try to give them a good time with music; all human beings want to relax. I try not to be too wordy... I'll get them singing, running around, laughing, working in groups to make up songs, recording them and playing them back to each other, and then voting for the best one. At the beginning of the session I take a photo of them all, and they're often stiff and posed, unsmiling. I take another one at the end and of course they're all laughing and relaxed, and we compare the two and discuss what has happened. And they all laugh. "Do I need to say more?" I say to the teachers. "Don't you want this for your children?" After singing you've

aerated your blood and the oxygenated blood is in the brain; you feel alert and ready to face whatever comes next. A seven-year-old will come out of this singing lesson happy and go into the next one, maths or whatever it might be, confident, lightened, her brain at ease, and she'll really be able to focus and concentrate.

I once went to a school to do some singing CPD for a primary staff, and there was a teacher who was a tough nut, she was very resistant to what we were doing, and her attitude was spreading to the others. There was a lot of whispering behind hands, but as a professional, you can't react, so I kept going, kept trying to encourage her. At one point I said to her, "Could you perhaps try to have a go? Just vocalise if you don't actually want to sing", and I suddenly realised that this woman was terrified, of herself, of her voice, of being humiliated. In the end I said, not looking at her, "One of the reasons why this training can be valuable is that everybody has to confront their own demons – you might think you sing well but you know you can't do the top notes, or maybe you don't sing at all. There's always a 'but' and everyone has to confront their buts." Then I turned to her and she burst out laughing and she said, "I haven't been very nice, have I?" And I said, "It's not about being nice. It's about understanding where the children are. All these feelings are ones you'll get in the classroom – you need to feel what the children will feel." When I went back a few weeks later this teacher was one of the most active and supportive in the group.'

As well as making children happy and relaxed, then, singing, with its need for deep breathing and upright posture, and its exercising of the abdominal muscles, has physiological effects too. These appear to prepare children well for the work they have to do sitting down with pens and pencils.

But there's something else really vital about singing, which is about the context in which it happens. Richard himself describes what originally motivated him to become the successful musician he is today:

'When I was six we started every day by belting out the hymns at assembly. The one I best remember is God Is Love, His the Care, and that bass line! Old Miss Roberts, she could play it quite well: it went bom bom bom bom and I used to shiver with excitement. There were 250 of us all belting it out. That's what turned me on to singing.'

This may have been about at least three things: the nature of that particular hymn, with its strong, simple melody and powerfully harmonised bass line, certainly; secondly, the emotional and physical sensation produced by the volume of noise of that number of people singing together around you; but there is also the social dimension of what happens when you are one of those 250 simultaneously singing people. Whether it's in a football or rugby ground or a church or at Glastonbury, the power of the shared singing experience is immense and has been well researched. For example, psychologist Susan Maury (2014) suggests that there are emotional, social and cognitive benefits for people who sing in groups, as well as increased empathy. From an evolutionary point of view, one of the reasons that humans have engaged in social singing for so many thousands of years may have been because singing helps promote the kind of group co-operative behaviour that societies need to survive.

The school community is another setting where the co-operative behaviour that good class or whole-school singing engenders is for everyone's benefit. Teachers can be made more confident singing leaders with a couple of hours' CPD, as we've seen, and once they have found their singing voices, they will definitely use them. When a school becomes a singing school, a choir can be started, again perhaps using a volunteer from the community to lead it, and there are many national organisations to help you with resources, such as the award-winning Sing Up (www.singup.org).

Listen out

With visual art, children can use the experience of looking at the work of other artists, at their subjects and techniques, as a stimulus to making their own art, and it is within their grasp to, say, use the same watercolour technique that J.M.W. Turner used, or make chalk drawings like Peter Paul Rubens did, or stencils like Banksy, even if the results decidedly remain children's art. But the abstract nature of music, and musical scores, and the required instrumental mastery means that for most primary-age children, there is no similarly direct linking thread between listening to classical or other complex music and performing it, or composing it, all three of which the curriculum requires. There are excellent online resources for introducing children to such a range of music, the BBC's

Ten Pieces (www.bbc.com/teach/ten-pieces), for example, which can help build this bridge. But, as imaginative and accessible as they are, even they demand a lot of a teacher who is not musically literate.

Just as we can learn visual literacy by spending time with images, interrogating them slowly and finding answers, we can do a parallel thing with music. It's harder, yes, because music takes place in time; each note or chord is there for a nanosecond and then moves on. It's more elusive for being abstract: without the safe prompts of word and image, we are in another world whose language, if it is an unfamiliar genre, we may feel we just don't understand. But good listening skills can help us learn this new language, quite apart from all the other ways they help to develop, among other things, language, empathy and concentration.

So we could start with the easiest thing of all, with sound, the raw material of music. And the most available sounds are those of the world outside. If you are a rural school, this might be dominated by natural sounds: birdsong, the noise of dogs, sheep or cattle, wind in trees, rain on the roof or windows, the crunch of footsteps through snow, and these more delicate sounds perhaps interrupted by the rumble of agricultural vehicles or a plane above. The soundscape of city schools will be much more thickly textured, dominated by traffic, and the noise of humans, animals or weather will need really focused listening to detect. Even a short period of this kind of close aural attention can be the start of something: listen to (in complete silence), record and play back two or three minutes of ambient sound outside. Notice its three-dimensional nature – the foreground sounds are louder than the more remote ones. Ask everybody what they heard before playing back the recording: there will be things that everyone caught, a siren or a yell, some that only a few detected, a distant train perhaps, and others that no one at all heard, maybe because it was so mundane – for example, a door slamming somewhere.

This recording can be played about with, slowed down or sped up. It can be the beginnings of a piece of music composed by a class or a group, where the sounds and rhythms are imitated by actual instruments – untuned or tuned percussion if there is no one who plays anything else; it can be part of a mixtape of ambient sounds at different times of day; it might provide the soundtrack to an animation; it could be illustrated digitally or with art materials, or stimulate creative writing… there are no limits.

Making such a recording is also a perfect preparation for listening to composed music that has also used or been stimulated by found sounds, either urban or rural: play Bang on a Can All-Stars' *Field Recordings* project or Edgard Varèse's 'Amériques', a representation of New York for a large orchestra, including police sirens, or John Adams' 'Short Ride in a Fast Machine', for example.

When children become accustomed to this kind of slow, attentive listening, their ears are tuned to exploring sounds and they will develop a vocabulary to discuss them and the way they are structured. Listening to short works becomes possible, especially when the listening is guided – for example: 'Halfway through this work listen out for the cow bells, spot the very quiet drumming moment and see how the music accelerates towards its end.' Many schools play music in class as a background to encourage a quiet working atmosphere and this can be a good, surreptitious way of familiarising children with the repertoire you want to introduce; the purist in me, however, wants to say that I'd definitely want 'foreground' listening as well. The practice of 'drawing' music is also widespread: that is giving children large pieces of paper and a range of drawing materials and asking them to draw what they hear. This can be representational – 'it sounds like water' or 'someone running – or more abstract marks can be made, in which case different marks can be used to convey loudness and softness, rhythm and timbre, and then you have the beginnings of notation. Drawing like this seems to be a useful way of focusing the listening, and it can also help in maintaining children's ability to draw spontaneously, which as we saw in the previous chapter is something that they are likely to lose if it's not attended to.

Music live

The moment children are used to listening to recorded music in a concentrated way is the moment to let them hear it live. If you're in a city, live music is not hard to find, from street buskers to orchestras in concert halls and everything in between. If you're more rural it might be about inviting musicians in. Either way, it can be an encounter that inspires and encourages, and may also identify early talent: star trumpeter Alison Balsom decided she wanted to play her instrument after being offered free lessons at her primary school when she was eight, and a year later she was taken to see famous trumpeter Håkan Hardenberger perform.

She remembers thinking the next day at school, 'Now that's what it's all about!' Similarly, Tess Bhesania, assistant head at Cleveland Road Primary School, told me about one of her violin-playing Year 6 girls, who was in a class taking part in the London Symphony Orchestra's education programme Discovery. They had been to the Barbican to perform on stage and stayed on later to watch the LSO perform. Tess told me, 'That girl said to me, "You know, Miss, I'm going to play with that orchestra one day…"'

The children from Cleveland Road would have been well prepared for this concert. They were lucky enough to be part of a pioneering and very well developed music education programme, which involves close connections with world-class professional musicians. But going out to hear music can be challenging if the conditions aren't right, partly because the conventions of listening to live music, especially classical music, can often be restrictive. Having to sit still and quiet and focus on something abstract is hard for everyone. I go to a lot of live music and my mind often drifts; my legs get restless or I want to have a conversation with my neighbour about something exciting in the music. Unless, perhaps through a local music education hub, you have a good working partnership with a performing organisation, it may be more appropriate to start with live music at school. Going back to the theme of auditing your wider school community for talent, Richard Frostick reminds us that, if you do, you're going to find that somebody in your staff team has learned an instrument, is still learning or is married to somebody who is. He tells the story of a school he visited where one of the lunchtime supervisors played the piano, well enough to play for assembly. Or the talent will be in the parent group: in his music centre, Richard discovered that the parents of one of the choir played in a Bolivian folk band and they now perform for the children at their Christmas party. Of course you may also have retired teachers in your community who would like nothing better than to contribute their musical skills to the life of your school.

Inviting a performing musician into school is, as you know, like inviting any other visiting teacher – it works best if they have really good communication skills. A good school performance should be no different from a good public performance: they both involve much more than artists standing and playing their instrument well. A performance is also about putting an audience at ease, about arousing their curiosity. It involves humour and eye contact, participatory elements, and playing instruments in a way that is compelling because it's so skilled and the artists are so caught up in the performing moment. And of course, a school performance works best when it's short, 30 to 40 minutes perhaps, and when the children are left wanting more.

Learning to play a tuned instrument

I've left this issue until last because, contrary to what you might expect, it's the last element to put in place when creating a musical school. You might argue that surely music teaching is about getting children to be competent musicians, to be musically literate (able to read musical notation) and able to play a sequence of notes on an instrument. But unless it's a keyboard, we're talking about producing notes by combining a number of motor and other muscular skills: for stringed instruments using two hands, one to make the note, the other to bow, and for woodwind or brass, a hand and demanding mouth control. Mastering these skills requires regular tuition and, even more important, regular, supervised practice, either at school, which has its own logistical challenges, or at home, something that can seem impossible for many families. And yes, to have every child playing an instrument would be an outstanding outcome, but in the real world, as you know all too well, resources have to be harvested. There is also an issue of entitlement. Is your aim to produce a few stars or do you want every child to learn musicianship through good class teaching and through singing? Or do you aspire to both?

But who will do the work?

Perhaps you have decided that music could move a bit closer to the centre of your school's creative life. If you are starting from a limited base, it's probably best to take a slow-burn approach. You may think you need some class singing as well as the whole-school variety. And you can appreciate the value of good class teaching of the elements of music. Later a choir could be started, and then you could move on to the idea of a rich offer of instrumental teaching, with private or small group lessons. When music is an everyday part of the school, the motivation to learn an instrument will also be keener. At that point, don't ignore the idea of recorder teaching. Recorders were traditionally taught in primary schools for the good reasons that children can produce decent results quickly on a tuned instrument, the instruments are cheap and robust, and without much trouble you can have the beginnings of a band or recorder consort.

We've mentioned using musicians from the community around you and how schools such as Cleveland Road have also looked further afield for rich music experiences by taking up provision offered by local music institution providers, either directly or through the local music education hubs. The National Plan for Music Education (NPME), set up in 2011, created the hubs for the following purposes:

a) *Ensure that every child aged 5–18 has the opportunity to learn a musical instrument (other than voice) through whole-class ensemble teaching programmes for ideally a year (but for a minimum of a term) of weekly tuition on the same instrument.*

b) *Provide opportunities to play in ensembles and to perform from an early stage.*

c) *Ensure that clear progression routes are available and affordable to all young people.*

d) *Develop a singing strategy to ensure that every pupil sings regularly and that choirs and other vocal ensembles are available in the area.*
(Department for Education, 2011)

So you should be able to achieve what you need to do with the help of such external resources. The Music Mark External Services Directory (available at: www.musicmark.org.uk/members) can tell you which providers exist in your area. You could outsource all your teaching to a local provider – the Buckinghamshire Learning Trust or Durham Music Service, for example, or your local equivalent – but of course you will also want some quality assurance. You can be confident that long-established and well-evaluated programmes such as Discovery at the London Symphony Orchestra, mentioned on page 51, will deliver, and of course you can ask your headteacher colleagues who have successful music teaching programmes. However, as when reading a TripAdvisor review, you should always bear in mind that everyone's recommendations are based on their own priorities, experiences and standards, and I would definitely want to witness what was on offer myself. As well as checking the testimony on the providers' own promotional materials, I'd want to see the quality of the teaching (as opposed to the skill of the musicians) and I'd be keen to hear what children had to say about it. I would also want to find out whether the offer was flexible enough to meet my school and curriculum's own particular needs. The downside of this kind of provision is that it is more an add-on, less close to the heartbeat of the school and less able to contribute to enriching the rest of the curriculum.

Another approach for enrichment, as opposed to full delivery, might be to look around at local venues or performing groups and see whether they have a learning and participation officer or community engagement officer, or if not, go to the top and ask the director what they could do for you. Some of the most successful arts education programmes and projects have started from speculative requests by heads or teachers, and, since so much arts funding of all kinds is dependent on (or directed towards) learning provision, it is always in arts institutions' interests to listen to education professionals.

Here is an example of local provision that might not be the first place you'd think of turning to if it was nearby. Garsington Opera in Buckinghamshire has a learning and participation offer, now an established initiative, whose mission is to enrich people's lives through opera. Opera is so often seen as an elitist art form, with silly plots performed in a foreign language by people singing in a false and unnatural style in front of posh audiences. What could it offer primary schools? The answer is that opera is just heightened storytelling and so children have no problem with it. This company, along with most of the other larger ones in the UK, regularly proves that with the right choice of repertoire, and in the hands of skilled animateurs this art form is genuinely accessible. It can teach musical skills, especially vocal, and theatre skills are an additional benefit. The really imaginative companies do two things: they familiarise children with an opera through school workshops; this normally culminates in a special, schools-only performance of the work on the main stage. At Garsington this is performed by singers in the company's young artists programme and the house is always full of youthful energy. The performance is followed by a backstage visit with a chance to talk to costume, make-up and other technical professionals.

Children in Years 5 and 6 who have enjoyed participating in this programme then get the opportunity to join the company's youth opera scheme, which takes place in the Easter and summer holidays; the nine- and ten-year-olds work with older students (up to the age of 13 and sometimes 21), so for primary-age children this offers a gentle introduction to the looming world of secondary school.

The operas for this company are always commissioned with young performers in mind. I watched a performance of *Eliza and the Swans* by John Barber (music) and Hazel Gould (words), directed by Karen Gillingham, with vocal coach Suzi Zumpe. With a team of creative artists like this, who really understand how children and young people operate, how much to challenge them, and how to give them heartfelt and luscious music to sing and act, the results on stage can be spectacular. Talking afterwards to the teachers who had volunteered to accompany the children during their holidays, it was clear that they hugely valued the opportunity for their pupils, said that they had discovered previously unknown talents in their classes and very much appreciated the performances as adults.

Another model of provision can be found in Aldeburgh, Suffolk, where the local primary school looked to the Britten-Pears Foundation (BPF) for help with delivering aspects of the music curriculum. The BPF is located on the site of the home of the 20th-century composer Benjamin Britten and his partner, the singer Peter Pears. The composer's house and garden as well as his archive can be visited. The school and the BPF together developed a programme that linked music into other curriculum areas such as history, art and science, and is delivered by the BPF's learning curator. This is a good example of creative collaboration through which both organisations extended ambitions.

So there's a lot on offer outside and much to do in school. The question is, then, what kind of person should have responsibility for ensuring that the music curriculum is delivered as is required, as every child deserves? Will it be the local provider, or an arts or music subject lead with an already heavy curriculum load? Or could you take on a full-time specialist music teacher as Feversham Academy has done?

> **Case study 2**: Feversham Primary Academy, Bradford
>
> Feversham Primary Academy has been much written about in the press as an example of a school that has turned itself round through its arts curriculum, with a special focus on music. It went from being in Ofsted special measures to rated 'good' in just a year. Curious to see what was driving this success, I took the

train to Bradford on a blustery day in March and walked from the station up the hill, through edgy streets of small, bleak terraces, where rubbish blew about like autumn leaves. As I was buzzed through the steel gates, the first thing I saw on the wall of the school building was a banner saying 'talk to your child', which seemed like a good place to start.

I met the head Naveed Idrees in his office. He had an air of busy-ness: not only is he headteacher of the school but he is also in the system leaders group that supports the other local schools in AET, the multi-academy trust that Feversham is a part of; on any day he might be addressing the House of Lords about education through music or talking to other music education organisations in London, so he is often out of the building. However, he tells me, in the five years of his headship he has built a strong middle management team. There are phase leaders who come through the ranks and all the core functions are distributed to phase leaders and subject lead teachers. 'They get on very well without me now,' he says. I asked him why he had decided to go for a creative curriculum:

When I arrived at Feversham we were in special measures and had been a sink school for 25 years. No one wanted to send their children here; the staff were demoralised and the children were not learning. So my starting point was 'it's not working'. Behaviour was atrocious; we're in a high crime area and the children have siblings who are in gangs. It was a complete disaster and the school was full of people from the Department for Education and consultants. You went into any class and there was a consultant there and what were they doing? More English and more maths. Why? Because we were so far below the national standard. It was then that we decided that that way of learning was not working. So we stopped all these consultants coming to school and said, 'We don't need you... you're creating a dependency culture for my staff and you've been doing this for 20 years and nothing has changed.' Then we asked ourselves: 'What do we think education is for? What is the point of children coming to school if it's just to pass the SATs?' That isn't the point – the point is for them to

Illustration 1.1: © 1974 Quentin Blake. *How Tom Beat Captain Najork and His Hired Sportsmen*, by Russell Hoban and illustrated by Quentin Blake. Reproduced by permission of Walker Books Ltd, London SE11 5HJ, www.walker.co.uk.

Illustration 1.2: *Argentinian Pucarás at Stanley Airstrip* (1982), by Linda Kitson. © Linda Kitson.

Illustration 1.3: *Portrait of Giovanni (?) Arnolfini and His Wife*, by Jan van Eyck. © The National Gallery, London.

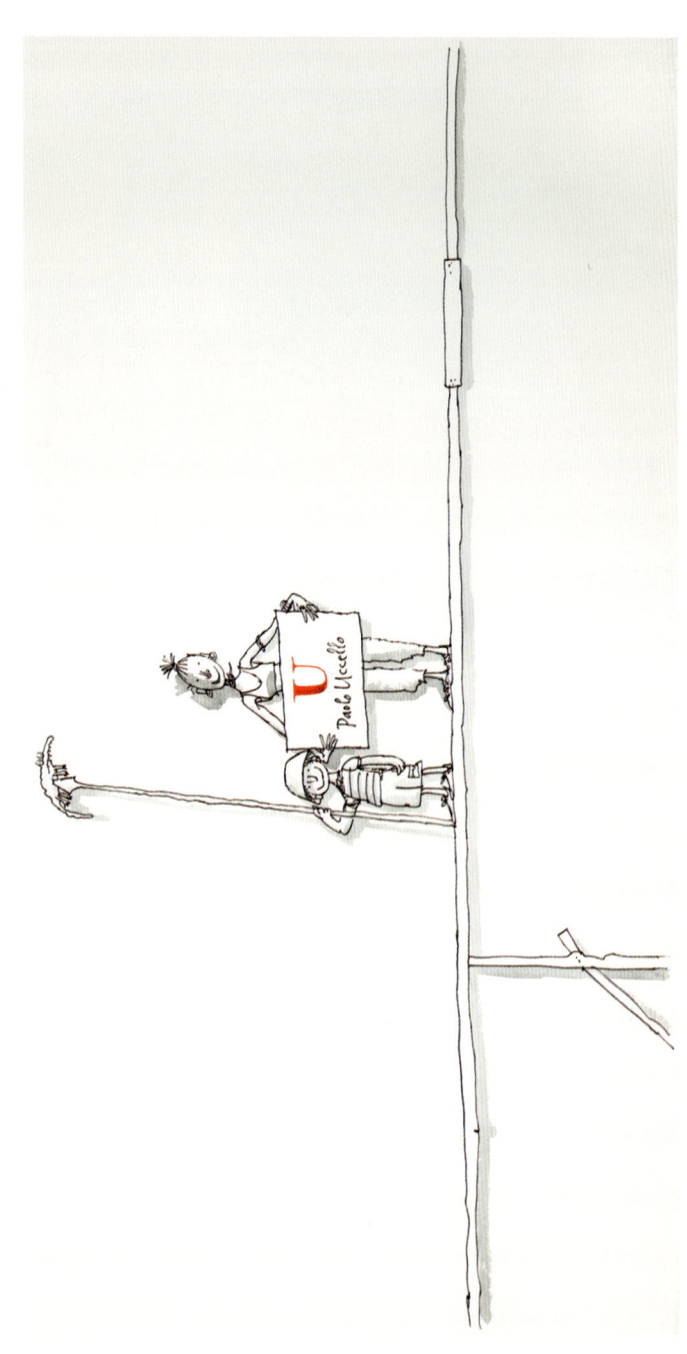

Illustration 2.1: Museum label for an artwork by Uccello from the National Gallery exhibition 'Tell Me a Picture', by Quentin Blake. © Quentin Blake.

Illustration 2.2: *The Long Slide*, by Mr and Mrs Smith. Reproduced with kind permission from the Estate of Ray Smith.

Illustration 2.3: *The Long Slide*, by Mr and Mrs Smith. Reproduced with kind permission from the Estate of Ray Smith.

Illustration 2.4: Public art, including *The Scallop*, a sculpture by Maggi Hambling (© Education Images/UIG via Getty Images), the village sign for Boxford, Suffolk (© Alison Avery), and a lizard sculpture (© Dominic Latham-Koenig).

Illustration 2.5: *Bacchus and Ariadne*, by Titian. © The National Gallery, London.

Illustration 2.6: *Perseus Turning Phineas and His Followers to Stone*, by Luca Giordano. © The National Gallery, London.

Illustration 2.7: *Kitchen Scene with Christ in the House of Martha and Mary*, by Diego Velazquez. © The National Gallery, London. Bequeathed by Sir William H. Gregory, 1892.

Illustration 2.8: *Incommunicado*, by Mona Hatoum. © Mona Hatoum. Courtesy of Arnolfini, Bristol (Photo: Edward Woodman).

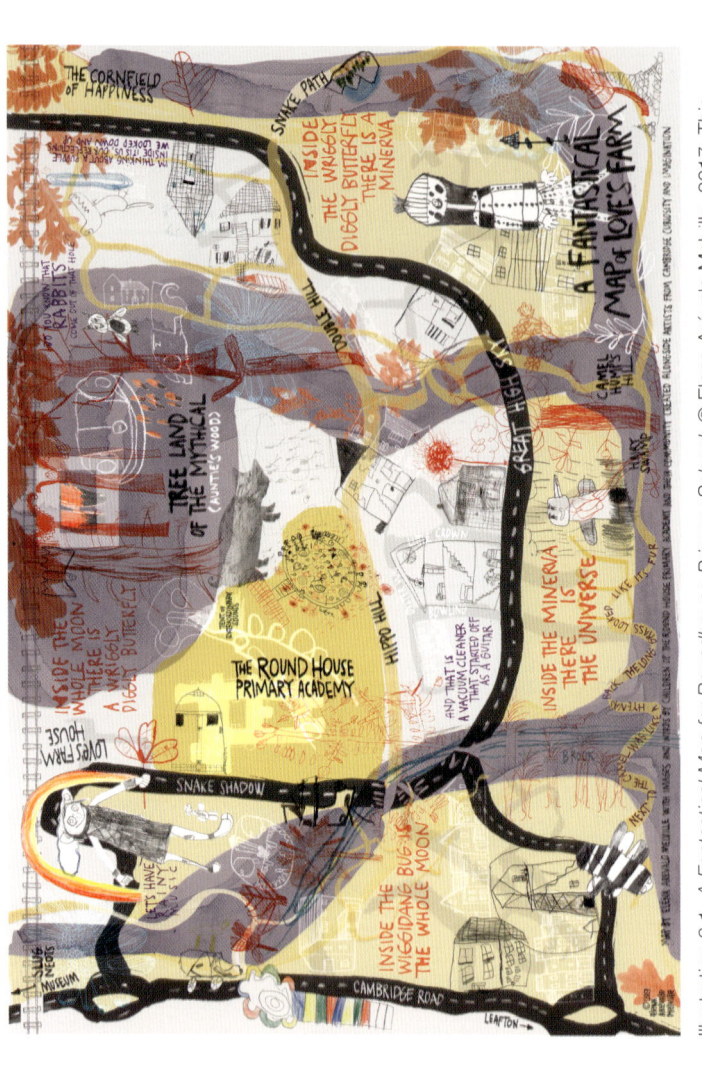

Illustration 6.1: *A Fantastical Map for Roundhouse Primary School*. © Elena Arévalo Melville, 2017. This map, based on a residency in the school with artists Filipa Pereira Stubbs, Sally Todd and Helen Stratford, is one of a series commissioned by Cambridge Curiosity and Imagination for their Fantastical Cambridgeshire programme. With thanks to all the children in the school, their educators and the wider community.

Illustration 7.1: *The Wilton Diptych. English or French (?). Richard II Presented to the Virgin and Child by His Patron Saint John the Baptist and Saints Edward and Edmund.* © The National Gallery, London. Bought with a special grant and contributions from Samuel Courtauld, Viscount Rothermere, C.T. Stoop and the Art Fund, 1929.

Illustrations 7.2 and 7.3: Display boards at Windmill Hill School. © Mark Hazzard.

grow and be ready for life – so we decided that we were not going to do yet more English and maths because our children come in with little or no English language, or even home language either, nothing. The richness is not there; the parents can't provide it at all. The children can't even sit still. Our analysis was that the learning behaviours need to be right first, so we said we need to do more arts and music, because music (and drama) teaches you discipline, pattern spotting, resilience, peace and calm, among many other things. The second question we needed to ask was what our assumptions were about what a child is. Is a child a robot whose brains need to be filled? No, and that's an interesting thing: the unspoken assumption about the way we're operating, which tells us about our current model of what education is, and what we understand a child to be.

And so the idea was born that we'd make the curriculum more creative. It was a conscious effort at the time. It's something that grew organically and engaged the children. We started by employing a specialist drama teacher on supply and we developed them and nurtured them. Then Jimmy Rotheram (the music co-ordinator) also came in as a supply. Previously each class would have half an hour per week for one term in the year: someone would come in and do a half-hour singing or instruments session (through the local music hub). It wasn't even for the whole year, and we wanted to give them more. So I did advertise for a music teacher but I didn't get anywhere; there are musicians and teachers but not combinations of the two, so we started with supply and Jimmy came in one day per week.

Jimmy had been secondary trained and was teaching A-level music so decided he needed to learn a system that was more suited to primary children; he was also looking for something that was going to help them sing in tune. He says:

When I started here four years ago there were only two or three children in each class who could sing in tune and there was no sense of pulse or rhythm. None of the basics were there. The school had been starved of music – and with 98 per cent of the children being from a Pakistan Muslim culture in which music is often prohibited, there wasn't a culture of making music at home either. I started teaching Years 5 and 6 in a tiny space, much of which was taken up by the piano. The kids loved the lessons and were highly engaged but at this stage I was merely a children's entertainer. My research drew me to the Kodály approach, which was great because it's so holistic (in fact the Kodály philosophy 'always a joy, never a torture' is applied throughout the school in all subjects). It develops everything from motor co-ordination to social skills and that's consciously embedded in the programme. What appealed to me at first was that I learned that everyone can sing soh and me in tune and that music is about natural speech patterns – like how your mum calls you to dinner. I tried it out with the children and it's true! Everyone can sing soh and me. From there we went on to add la me ray doh and that was the beginning of it! It worked like magic and there was the fun element too. You play lots of games and children don't realise that they're learning these advanced music skills, but by the time they're in Year 5 or 6 they can do everything, because it's holistic musically as well. It's not just bringing out good music readers; they can also improvise, they can compose...

I asked Jimmy about children learning instruments from very young:

If you give children instruments too early, it's like building on sand. It should all be about musicianship at first. I do sometimes start people early if they show a lot of potential. There was a little girl who got out all the chime bars one day and arranged them in thirds, without any input from me, and then she played them with really good rhythms. She was in Year 3 and she became a really outstanding drummer. At Key Stage 2 we have 80 children learning instruments, which we've bought. I bring in peripatetic teachers and they give private lessons, which we pay for. We've now got trumpets, drums, keyboards and guitars, and by Year 4 most children can read music. Music is definitely not just an add-on and I support class teachers to get music into the curriculum so that it's in the topics covered. Every topic has a song to go with it. We also have a one-hour music assembly each week, which usually features a guest musician (I have a weekly budget of £25 for this).

At this point, Jimmy sighs about what so often happens in primary school music:

Music is supposedly compulsory in schools, but primary schools have been getting away with not delivering it, delivering it unmusically, or outsourcing the music education in their schools and abdicating from their responsibility to teach music well, even though the real 'window of opportunity' for potentially significant neurological developments and true pitching is about three to six years old. People like Dr Anita Collins and Dr Katie Overy, among others, have done significant research on the effects of music on the developing mind and have demonstrated how it can help children with ADHD, dyslexia, autism and other special needs.

So to see what Jimmy thinks *should* go on in primary music, I visit a Reception class music session in the large, bright music room. Well-kept instruments line the walls; an 'artistic TA', as Jimmy describes her, has covered the many display boards in bold, music-related images. A nursery assistant is at the piano and tells me how she wished she'd had this kind of music education when she was little. To Jimmy's great annoyance, the class arrives late – precious minutes from the half-hour class have gone forever – but when the children do arrive, several of them walk in, quiet and orderly, some already singing the song they had learned the previous week. The class teacher and teaching assistant join in the circle and the children are fully engaged in the session, which involves singing, soft toys (young children will often rather sing to a toy or puppet than to an adult), moving about and a lot of laughing. One child, a boy with severe autism, does not co-operate except in the singing: he makes a beautiful sound, completely in tune. Jimmy explains that this is the one area of school life where this child can make sense of his world, which is so full of sensory confusion.

Naveed takes me on a tour of the school, where it is clear that although music was an early building block in his bid to provide a rich learning environment for the children of this truly deprived community, it wasn't the only factor. The school is full of arts spaces – a drama room, which the drama specialist has properly resourced with props and costumes, and two libraries including a soft room for relaxed individual reading. There's a forest school in which Naveed plans to create a sculpture park after the school has made a visit to the Yorkshire Sculpture Park near Wakefield. We passed a Year 6 class, normally at this stage of the year in full bootcamp mode, but this class were making Greek temples out of clay…

Back in Naveed's office, we talk about resourcing this kind of curriculum. The school has the same funding formula as other local schools but less of their budget is spent on staff: 59 per cent as opposed to the average of 75 to 80 per cent. They spend almost nothing on supply teaching and Naveed is the only non-teaching member of the senior leadership team. He also has an untypical attitude to the employment of teaching assistants, believing that when you analyse how their time is used, you find out that they spend 20 minutes of each lesson listening to the class teacher. So he has very few TAs and has instead started a graduate programme, in which he recruits specialists for two years, offering them a range of teaching roles and opportunities to shadow teachers. If at the end of the two years the senior leadership team feels they're ready, they'll be rewarded with Qualified Teacher Status. The scheme is highly popular, often attracting 100 applications for one post.

Naveed also feels strongly that the arts would get the place they deserve in the curriculum if they were assessed not by testing but instead by looking at the number of hours devoted to them, and the kinds of experiences offered to children. 'We need a measure,' he pleads. 'Indicators of an enriched curriculum, including a pupil survey and evidence of timetabling – and quantify that to a figure. Schools should need to feel competitive about this.'

I asked Naveed, as I have asked all the heads I have met, whether his wholesale embrace of an arts-rich curriculum meant that he had had an arts background himself. 'Not really,' was his answer. 'At my own primary school we maybe had a bit of guitar and songs.' Then he paused a bit and said:

> *I've always been more interested in the wider human angle – in developing yourself holistically – you're not just a brain, you're a soul, a spirit as well. I hadn't really thought of it, but I've got spirituality in my background. I come from the Sufi tradition – connecting with the mystery of creation, something beyond yourself, and that's what's missing from our education system; that's the key to everything – to your motivation, to your mental health, to your progress – and I see music and arts developing the spirit. I feel that the system is encouraging people to destroy that element, something that existed in primary schools for many years. We have children from three to 11; that's a long time. We know the community here and we're trying to plug the gaps. We're trying to turn these children into good citizens and happy people – so this life experience, this richness, where are they going to get that if not here?*

Each school exists in its own context and with its own history and so is not directly comparable with another one. But the general learning from schools like Feversham and from the wide experience of specialists such as Richard Frostick could perhaps be distilled down to a few pointers: first, take time! The decision to build an arts-rich curriculum at Feversham was clear and strategic, but its implementation was fairly organic and dependent on employing, nurturing and training specialist teachers. The person you find for the music job might have great skill as a musician and enthusiasm to work in primary education but they may still need further training: musicians who are also trained teachers are, by the nature of their expertise, likely to come from the secondary sector and will need support and time to transition to working with very young children. Once appointed, such a music teacher might also need additional training in musicianship programmes aimed at the primary age group, or you may find a musician who is not actually a trained teacher and they will definitely need those skills. After starting at Feversham, Jimmy Rotherham was trained in the Kodály method and attended what he described as a 'life-changing' summer school run by the British Kodály Association. There are other systems such as the Dalcroze, Gordon, Orff and Suzuki, and the Kodály-based Jolly Music scheme can even be used by non-specialist staff in the Early Years. Similarly, The Voices Foundation is a singing-led programme that focuses on teacher training.

Second, make the most of the music teacher. Ensuring that the music specialist is a well-integrated member of your teaching team will mean that everyone can benefit from their skills. Jimmy shares his expertise with the whole staff: they become more musically literate themselves and so music extends into other parts of the curriculum, with Jimmy providing teachers with songs that link to cross-curricular themes or topics.

The third is if your plan to boost the arts does not run to employing a full-time music specialist, look around outside to see who can help you best. Who are the people, organisations or providers who can best help you do what you want to do for your school? Starting with a competent and inspiring person or a small music organisation may in the end be more fruitful than buying an expensive off-the-shelf package from a big provider, however less time-consuming the latter might be.

Chapter 4
Dance

> *'The intelligence of dance is far superior to intellectualism – the body is more honest and direct.'* (Akram Khan, in Jaggi, 2010)

We may not watch much broadcast TV together as a nation any more but we're currently rather obsessed with watching people dance on it. Ten million of us watched the first live episode of *Strictly Come Dancing* in September 2018 (Davies, 2018). Is that because we love a competition? Because we have a fascination in how much interest develops between the dancing pairs? Or because it's heartening to see people making progress (and failing by falling too)? Or is it also because the people on the floor really do look as if they are experiencing extreme enjoyment? Because the smiles on the competitors' faces when they finish their routines are so genuine? Keep those images in mind as we think about the role dance can play in primary schools.

Dance versus PE

Dance is a part of the National Curriculum, but, as you know, its curriculum big brother is PE. Both are about learning to move the body with control, but in many other ways, as disciplines, they are miles apart. PE and sports are primarily about learned, logical routines, and about how children extend their agility, balance and co-ordination in them or in team games or individual sports. There, PE also often points towards competition and strategies for winning.

Yes, dance at its simplest can be about learning a pattern of moves, and it can make use of PE skills such as running, jumping, throwing and catching, but many forms of dance, including ballet and what is known as modern dance, have a fundamentally creative aim; dance is the physical expression of a whole person, where their feelings, personality and understanding of a narrative are driving the movement; and, unless we're thinking about solo performance, dance is fundamentally a collaborative art; it depends totally on opening up to and receiving other people's physical presences. Normally it also involves 'collaborating' with music: listening to it, being inspired by it, and moving to its beat or against its beat. For this reason, dance and PE are strange bedfellows but in schools they are currently funded through the PE and sport premium. Of course, in one way this could be seen as a good thing – it does keep dance in the picture – but in another it often means that dance is being delivered by a sports coach or teacher. Tori Drew, Education Manager at One Dance UK (the only subject association for dance), feels that the introduction of the PE and sport premium has led to the creation of many sports teaching companies without any expertise or experience within dance, but when these organisations deliver the dance curriculum, the offer can often be unsatisfactory. This is because the coaches involved frequently lack specialist dance skills. The dance lesson can end up as little more than a beefed-up gymnastics session, with a couple of balances and a forward roll being described as a dance.

Barriers

Sometimes the dance box is ticked through after-school or lunchtime clubs, where coaches are brought in to teach Zumba, Wake-Up! Shake Up!, street and similar dance styles. Apart from the fact that not all children are engaging with it, this, says Tori Drew, is a limiting approach to dance because it doesn't involve creative tasks, is heavily teacher-led and doesn't offer a range of styles. Dance as a subject is also increasingly being used in an instrumental way to tackle obesity, in particular obesity in girls: according to the Department for Digital, Culture, Media and Sport (2017), more five- to ten-year-old girls (48.6 per cent) choose to dance than boys (11.2 per cent). While she feels it's encouraging that dance is being used to support a more active and healthy lifestyle, Tori believes strongly that dance should be offered to both girls and boys equally. Boys and girls co-operating creatively and respecting each other is, after all, a good citizenship lesson too.

In this context, two other questions arise around whether and how dance might be included in the curriculum: those concerning disability and faith. As far as disability goes, the community dance movement has grown in this country over the last 40 years and has led to the formation of many inclusive dance companies, including for example Candoco, who have demonstrated how possible it is for everyone to dance. As regards faith, as Lyn Paine (2014), the respected dance teacher and trainer, says, when you teach in the diverse society that we have in the UK, you need to be aware that there are often 'misconceptions about the kind of dance that schools promote'. These may stem from a 'belief that popular social dance forms are not morally or spiritually acceptable'. However, Lyn says, 'As a teacher, you have a responsibility to articulate what you do in dance and why you value it.'

Tori Drew has an illustrative story in this connection: she was working on a secondary school project in Birmingham. The participants were all Islamic girls who loved dancing: 'I had done some dance with them,' Tori explains. 'And I had managed to get them a performance opportunity. At first they said they couldn't do this because it was against their religion: there would be males in the audience and so the girls would need to wear the hijab, which would prevent them doing this particular dance. But in the end they did perform it, without headscarves, to a mixed audience. That was down to the PE teachers who worked really hard, sharing with the families, explaining that the hijab would get in the way.'

Are there other barriers to giving dance an honoured place within the PE curriculum, and to having it taught by professionals in the art, rather than the sport, of dance? Or even for it to be taught by class teachers? I have sometimes perceived a lack of enthusiasm for the subject among non-specialist teachers who might otherwise advocate for it. Perhaps it's that unless they themselves are out-of-school dancers, they are reluctant to take part in dance, so they don't always have an emotional (sometimes also conceptual) understanding of the benefits that dance can bring. As Tori says, 'Dance involves your body being on show' and that is a big turn-off for many of us. But as we know, showing their bodies off by moving them is something that most young children do all the time, so perhaps we can start our thinking there.

Tori's argument, again one that I have come across many times in my school visits around the country in connection with all the other arts, is that teachers may not want to 'stand up and do beautiful ballet' (or perform beautiful music or make beautiful sculpture) in front of a class, but they *can* spark children's own physical or other creativity through the use of keywords and terminology to springboard ideas. In the case of dance: how can you travel slowly or quickly, or in a jagged way? How can you make that group more interesting? 'Teachers need to be aware,' Tori says, 'that dance can be very student-led and that's where the best dance happens; it really is about independent learning, something that dance enables so well.' We'll hear more about this in the case study on page 68.

Dance for all

So dance stimulates children's own natural creativity in the thing that's most familiar to them: their own bodies. Children are used to expressing themselves in words but in dance you can say to a child, 'Can you be a dinosaur?' and she won't need to know a factual answer, or be too logical, but she will truly be developing her own imaginative resources to recreate a dinosaur with her body (and then maybe later she will want to know more about dinosaurs). Tori believes, 'It really does involve something different from the usual ways of working and those kinds of skills are what the next generation of web designers and other creative people will need.'

Dance, along with visual arts and music, is not dependent on words, and so is accessible to a very high percentage of children, including those with a variety of special needs. We have mentioned disability but it is also enjoyable to children who struggle to express themselves with words, because of restricted or delayed language development, and it can have powerful effects on children who have difficulties with concentration. The story of Akram Khan, the dancer and choreographer whose words head this chapter, is an instructive one: he was a hyperactive three-year-old whose mother had the imagination to introduce him to folk dance, which he could do with great facility. Khan sees his subsequent school days as a time where his identity became invisible: he felt he was 'a shadow – even my teacher didn't know I was in the class' (Khan, in Jaggi, 2010), that is, until he won a school disco competition with a Michael Jackson 'Thriller' routine. Khan shone in a disco competition, but he might have had even greater self-confidence and success in the rest of the curriculum if there had been timetabled dance classes where his teachers and peers could have seen him for who he was: a talented dancer with a promising future. One of the messages of this book is that primary teachers, spending as much time with their classes as they do, knowing each child as they do, have a unique opportunity, a responsibility, I would argue, to identify and foster every child's inborn interests and talents. So often these are in fact to be found in or through the arts.

Dance then, being both creative and accessible, links with wellbeing, clearly now a topical theme for school leaders. The World Health Organization (2014) defines wellbeing as the state 'in which every individual realizes his or her own potential, can cope with the normal stresses of life, can work productively and fruitfully, and is able to make a contribution to her or his community'. And one way to start to achieve this is by being able to work things out for yourself, not just with your head, like getting a sum right in maths or spelling a word correctly, but figuring out and performing a sequence with your body in space. Think of the value of the kind of 'body rightness', which, perhaps even if you're naturally a bit shy, you might then perform in front of your classmates and get a clap for. Or doing the same thing after you've had a bad day, rowed with your mum in the morning, had a fight in the playground, or got into trouble for messing about in class. Tori talks about a time when she was a dance teacher herself and had a famous pre-warm-up routine, which was to ask the students to stand tall. Standing tall, she says, 'offers people so much. It's that sense of being open, looking up and out, looking at an audience.' This is a technique she has used particularly in her work with young offenders, which is about giving them the self-respect they so lack.

The way that creative dance depends on collaboration is also relevant here. Dance practitioners working in schools will usually get children working in groups to create dance sequences that can then be put together to make a bigger work. In these groups everybody has a voice and everybody has to be heard. But sometimes in a group you have to let your idea go in favour of a better one, or you have to be the person to convince everyone else that your idea is the one to go with. So you may have to argue your case, with your body as well as with words. You are developing listening skills and resilience in the face of disappointment, and learning how to be a team member and perhaps also how to lead.

The last benefit is one that we've already looked at but one that dance lends itself to especially well, and that's the idea of working in a crosscurricular way on whole-school themes or projects.

Tori is often invited into schools to help with this – for example, she worked with a school in the West Midlands, who brought her in for a year to do CPD across the school. She spent six weeks in each class, inventing the dance element for general themes, such as 'the rainforest'

Dance **67**

or 'under the sea'. She taught them dance actions and dynamics, and gave each teacher her lesson plan. Together they worked on joining up dance with the rest of the curriculum, and by the last week she was in school, the teachers had understood the principles, and had taken on future planning and delivery for themselves. 'I now feel confident to teach dance' was how one of the class teachers summed up in her evaluation of the programme. Tori mentioned an additional and unexpected outcome of such cross-curricular work, which teachers had reported back to her: 'Learning can really happen through dance; in a cross-curricular project about buildings the teachers were amazed at how much, through dance, children remembered.' The muscle memory involved in dance cued children to recall the other non-dance elements of the project.

The value of dance within a cross-curricular setting, as well as its ability to identify talent, were two of the strong focuses for Cleveland Road Primary School, our next case study.

Case study 3: Cleveland Road Primary School, Ilford, Essex

By the time I met Tess Bhesania (assistant headteacher and curriculum leader) and Katie Alexander (dance instructor) in a bright, cosy office, I had already made my way through many of the long corridors that crisscross this large school (there are nearly 1,000 children on roll at the time of writing). Every square centimetre along the route was covered with an endless variety of arts-related displays in many media. Tess explained that when she assumed her curriculum-lead post at Cleveland, her brief from the headteacher, Veena Naidoo, was to build an arts-rich curriculum (including dance) that would meet the needs of the children: it would inspire a commitment to lifelong learning, motivate pupils and enable them to become independent and confident learners. Through this curriculum they would become empowered to interpret the world around them, make sense of their experiences and express themselves effectively, creatively and imaginatively.

Tess began:

All the subjects were taught separately at the time. Music, history, geography and art were all planned discretely and there

wasn't much connectivity between them. We thought that if we were to create a more linked curriculum it would lead to deeper learning. The children would be able to spend more quality time exploring a theme and applying their understanding in different areas of the curriculum. The children would learn, for example, how great art, music, dance and literature are all informed by the historical period in which they are created and by the experiences of the artist, musician, choreographer, author or poet.

We set up opportunities in which pupils could, say, read a novel set during World War One and use their history lessons to help them make sense of what the characters are experiencing. They could then translate this knowledge and understanding within other subjects – for example, by creating a piece of modern, abstract dance. In doing this, the children are required to apply what they have learnt imaginatively and their learning begins to take new directions; they start to see links and connections between ideas, experiences, people and places. They begin to ask big questions about their homes, their communities, their beliefs and their own place in the world.

This kind of planning allows us to spend longer and go deeper – and then the learning stays with you. If you have a journey that has a narrative thread upon which children can hang their learning, they're going to retain it for longer; it's going to be more memorable to them and so it will mean more. And in dance, it's the kind of learning that is also collaborative.

Katie adds:

Dance brings the class closer together: if you think about it, throughout their primary school stage children are with the same children in class; working together in such a physical way is a way for them to learn about each other in a completely different way than they do in maths or English. If you and I were in Year 4 doing that World War One project,' she adds, *'and a teacher asked us to go out into the hall and explore what it felt like to traipse through a trench but using dance movements, we'd have a really different relationship with each other, a deeper understanding of each other, which of course will feed into how we'll interact in the playground, in the classroom, at lunchtime.*

Dance

Another telling example where dance cross-fertilised learning was connected with books. Curriculum planning at Cleveland always starts with a book, as it does in many schools: one per term for older children, and two for the younger ones. *Rooftoppers* by Katherine Rundell is a wonderful piece of imaginative storytelling about Sophie, who was left as a one-year-old floating in the English Channel in a cello case after a shipwreck. As she tries to track down her mother, whom she believes to be a cellist living in Paris, Sophie has a hair-raising adventure on the rooftops of the French capital. Katie explains how they linked it to the dance curriculum:

With that book we tried to hook children in at the beginning, and there's always quite a lot of mystery, so we started with a circus skills day (I'm originally trained in circus) and we brought in tight wires and other equipment. At this point in the story we needed to think: what's the important thing about running about on rooftops? And the answer was 'balancing', so that was where our learning was going to go. As the book went on, we constantly said to the children, 'Think back to that day at the beginning... why might we have done that?' Eventually when we got to the rooftop scene in the story they said, 'We've got it! We understand!' By having them balance on tight wires we had allowed them to feel in their bodies what it would be like to balance on those rooftops.

Tess added:

In experiencing their day of circus skills, the children began to understand the importance of teamwork and of trust – the understanding developed on day one of the journey had two big effects. The children were hooked! They were inspired to read the story and eager to follow the journey of the character (so much so that they followed her all the way to Paris!); the children were also able to empathise more with the characters. When Sophie takes her first steps onto the rooftops, she needs to place her trust in young Matteo, an orphan whose life is walked upon a tightrope. Having experienced that sense of danger for themselves, the children were able to understand what Sophie and Matteo were experiencing and relate this to their own lives.

So the curriculum is planned on a very wide arc, which dance can serve at any point. Katie is Cleveland Road's second dance instructor and she feels she has benefited from the spadework done by her predecessor, Emma Bellerby, who, as Lyn Paine advises, managed to convince the school's (mainly but not solely Muslim) families of why their children should dance. When she arrived, dance was a sensitive area for some: only girls wanted to do it, and she got letters from parents saying, 'My child shouldn't be dancing in school.' But over four years, attitudes have shifted. By 'going gently', Tess says, hearts and minds have been won over and the school has 'opened the community's heart' to what's possible through dance. Now, boys are as keen as girls and are often so good that they raise aspirations within the peer groups. Even more significantly, Tess thinks that children now see dance as a possible future career. One Year 6 girl developed a passion for ballet and modern dance after being introduced to it through the school dance lessons and a school visit to see the English National Ballet perform at Sadler's Wells. Before this girl left, Tess offered her guidance, pointing her towards Wayne McGregor and other companies she might get involved with – something her family weren't in a position to do. With the help of her primary school's curriculum, this girl had found a vocation.

Katie also talks about how this kind of success can be tracked. She mentions a Year 3 pupil who was always 'out there, completely engaged, and she always has her hand up' in the dance class. It happened that Katie always taught this group when the class teacher was on PPA (planning, preparation and assessment). At the end of term when the performance they had been preparing took place, this girl was right in the middle of the front row, with a big solo. The teacher couldn't believe it and she told Katie that she had wondered why she had seen such a change in this girl over the last six weeks. Katie pointed out that they had started to work on their performance six weeks before. 'Obviously,' she acknowledges, 'there may have been other factors, but it was a wonderful moment of us both realising that there was a correlation between the improvement in her in-class behaviour and her growing confidence as a dancer.'

The socialising aspect of dance teaching was an additional benefit that Cleveland Road began to become aware of. Katie remembered a child in Reception:

He was a little boy who, when he first came to school, refused to take off his bag and coat, and spent the whole day in Reception waiting to go home. Gradually he began to watch the dance lesson from the door; then he actually came into the hall; next his bag came off and another day he did a jump; and soon after he put his hand up for the first time, and then, in no time at all, every morning he'd come in and ask, 'Is it dance today?' After that he could manage school and we always put him in different groups for dance, so he got to know other children and that helped him to make friends.

The last thing that Tess and Katie wanted to emphasise about dance at Cleveland Road is the methodology used by Katie and its sometimes unexpected outcomes, because this way of working applies so well to all arts teaching:

The way we've run the dance class is very improvisational, exploratory and creative, and we've always been really open to the children in saying how similarly the lessons are run to how a professional dance company would operate. When making their work the children go through exactly this kind of process and then children start to feel as if they're professional, which I think is crucial: it gives them a feeling that this is something real and important. One of the things my predecessor, Emma, wanted to do was to make that connection in people's minds: that the arts don't have to be for and about adults. In school the arts, and dance in particular, can be a part of something else; there can be real synergy with another subject, dancing some science, for example. We started combining quite random things like [dance and science] together and creating a whole-school project with this in mind, and – this was the thing – in which every class was pupil-led in the learning. Each class was given two areas to combine. This became very important when children started to take ownership

72   The Arts in Primary Education

and make choices, which was terrifying for many of the teachers. They said, 'What if the children don't have any ideas? What do we do then?' But they got on with it anyway and later teachers started coming back with their results and what had surprised them was how many ideas the children did have – and it worked beautifully. That was the beginning of a shift; the staff began to feel a bit braver and each time the planning has got bigger and better.

Tess added:

This approach has had a positive impact on pupils and teachers across the school. We have seen children become more confident about taking the lead in their learning while teachers have become more interested in exploring processes and skills with the children and less concerned with the outcome. This has led to some amazingly creative and inspirational work, for example in the school's participation with the BBC Ten Pieces project and with the National Gallery's Take One Picture programme. The children are becoming more keen to experiment, take risks and try new things.

So now for dance, Katie says:

I'll always plan a session with the teachers or I'll go to their planning meeting and talk about progression. At these meetings, I'll jot down some suggestions because if you're not a dance practitioner, it's very hard to come up with dance ideas out of the blue, so you do need a bank of ideas. We have created a generic plan, which can either be mapped onto what the teachers come up with or to my suggestions. The teachers then go away and write the plan themselves: we find that it's very difficult to teach something you didn't write yourself. If teachers are integral in the planning stage then, when it comes to the lesson and we're team-teaching together, in a way it's constant CPD for them. This has led to some of them becoming really confident teachers of dance. Of course not all of them are, but that doesn't matter because they can come to me and ask me for any help. I'm always there to support them.

When I observed the Year 3 dance class, this is confirmed by the class teacher Kimberly, who I watch delivering the session with great conviction. Kimberly said:

Having someone like Katie to help is really beneficial – I had taught before but it was from a scheme. Now we discuss our topic together and I've got much better since working with her. The children in my class really enjoy dance, including all the boys. They've done it since Reception so now it's natural for them. From my own point of view, the other benefits include: firstly they work in groups, and they choose their own groups, so it's about the teamwork that happens as a result. Secondly, when they share with the rest of the class, they are now able to use a vocabulary for dance that they have learned during the classes. The other important thing is that the children have become more aware of their bodies and of how to use them: our warm-up activity today was painting the floor with your body and it was interesting to see how they each painted the floor completely differently: one with their elbows, one with their feet and so on. Lastly, after the lesson, they come into the next class happy. Not just happy but also keen to get on with their learning. We have guided reading after the dance lesson and they just get on with that; there's never a problem. But they're always super excited about dance: you hear them talking about it, and when we're getting ready for dance they'll say, 'Do you remember my movement from last week?'

The value placed on dance in this school can be seen in the curriculum time devoted to it: all children get an hour of dance per week, either with Katie (who teaches 12 classes per week) or with the class teacher and learning support assistant. At least one year group performs for the school each term and, as we saw, dance is also incorporated into whole-school projects. The school also offers an additional three hours per week of extra-curricular dance: one hour as an 'open-to-all' session and the other two for pupils in the Dance Company (who are identified as gifted and talented pupils), which enters several competitions every year.

> The arguments put forward by the leadership team in favour of dance are powerful, as was the evidence of the classes I watched.

If you are convinced, the desirable way forward is to treat dance as a discrete subject, as something that is more than and different to an extra bit of PE or a lunchtime club. Ideally it would be taught by a full- or part-time dance practitioner who could really work with the rest of the staff, as Katie Alexander said, 'delivering constant CPD'. But, failing that, and maybe as a way of dipping your toe into the dance world, you could start with CPD for your teachers or classes for your children, or you could aim to make the end-of-term or end-of-year show an especially ambitious one by including a strong dance element. These could all be delivered by a freelance instructor or an organisation such as Challenge 59. Many of the people who do this work are dance-trained to a high level but for various reasons don't actually want to be performers, and they often bring a high level of energy to a school community. You can find out about them and the teaching companies they are sometimes attached to through One Dance UK (www.onedanceuk.org/), who are national and so in a position to recommend contacts in your own locality, and they are always happy to provide support, guidance and CPD for dance in primary schools.

If you do embrace the art of dance at your school, you will be including a subject that easily enriches thematic or project-based work. It can turn itself to any area and throws new light on it. Your children will be involved in activities that are essentially collaborative: alongside dance and movement, they will be learning social and civic skills, which will benefit your community as well as the wider one outside. You will be offering some children who may not shine academically an opportunity to succeed in front of their peers and their significant adults, and you will be bringing in something that addresses the need to be physically active that all children have, especially in the Early Years. And coming out of a dance class, children experience that endorphin rush, that positive feeling in the body that leaves them fulfilled and ready to address whatever they have to do next.

Those are all excellent fringe benefits but most of all dance is valuable in itself because it connects physical movement to art in a unique way.

All the arts are curriculum subjects that really allow children to be themselves, but dance exemplifies this most perfectly: it's an art that challenges the disempowerment that children can feel in the face of a great body of knowledge that they understand they need to absorb to succeed in a test or to gain adult approval. As Kenyan educationist Tonee Ndungu (founder and COO of the Kytabu Centre for Education Innovations) says of education in Kenya, it's quite a universal concept: 'You go into a classroom in Kenya and there is nothing on the walls. That is because the teacher knows everything and I know nothing. What I do as a student doesn't matter.' (Greenwood Place, 2018)

In dance you matter completely because it's so obviously all about your person, in your body – the physical and emotional you, who can express yourself successfully in front of an audience and be affirmed by that. As has often been said about the arts, but especially about dance, they don't so much teach you about the subjects, they teach you about yourself. Surely, if as a school leader you want a school full of children who know themselves and feel as if they can succeed, dance is a subject you won't want to leave out.

Chapter 5
Drama

'Collective creative effort is the root of our kind of art.' (Constantin Stanislavski, 2013)

Of all the arts found in primary schools, drama is the one whose value and practice children understand most completely: after all, drama, the art of performing a fictional story by becoming a fictional character in it, is what they have been doing since toddlerhood when they first started engaging in imaginative play. As William, a Year 5 pupil at Springbank Primary School in Stoke, says: 'Usually you get your work on a piece of paper and it tells you what to do but in drama, it *shows* you what to do and it's a little bit different: it gets into your mind better than just words on a piece of paper.'

For adults, though, paying proper attention to a subject whose benefits, especially in the current educational climate, may seem elusive, is more of an ask. It's the area of the curriculum that, on a daily or weekly basis, is most about process and least about tangible outcome. Of course, you will be doing the big end-of-year show, a leavers' performance, a musical and a nativity or other Christmas-season play. You know how to produce the one-off event, with scripts to write, costumes, scenery and props to be made, and you appreciate the results when these things go well. But what does drama look like in your curriculum? Are there dedicated drama sessions? If not, what might be involved? Who would deliver the sessions? How much training would they need? What would have happened by the end of a drama lesson? Would it be something that could easily be measured or assessed and if so how? And this activity, which takes place in an empty space, with people sometimes opening up their feelings in quite raw ways, addressing what it means to be human, can it seem discomforting or embarrassing? Headteacher colleagues so often report hearing the staffroom comment, 'I don't do drama anymore', and it's not just because of the time commitment.

Instrumental or intrinsic?

There are two distinct ways of including drama in the primary curriculum but ideally they are strands that can be richly twined. The instrumental route is the commoner one, where drama skills are used to teach elements of the core curriculum. When you think about the intrinsic value of drama, on the other hand, you are talking about it being valued for what it is and all the elements and skills involved, rather than what it can do for a person or for other curriculum subjects.

Instrumental

Examples of the instrumental route might come under the general umbrella of what is known as process drama, where, as the name suggests, the process is the outcome. With its roots in the kind of imaginative play described above, process drama usually involves the teacher in role, in a devised scenario where children and teacher explore an issue together. This might be a moral or ethical situation, perhaps within the context of a history or geography unit, and children are asked to play different roles in order to think about a situation from different perspectives. A typical case might be based around the theme of migration: a story of refugees arriving in a new country is created, in which the notion of 'trying on someone else's shoes' can lead to a deep exploration of the many dimensions of this complex topic.

Teachers in role can also use well-known techniques such as hot-seat interviewing of significant figures of the past or present to animate history, science or maths. Having children interview a teacher in role, as say Florence Nightingale, Mary Seacole or Alan Turing, can be a far more powerful way of embedding knowledge than watching a video or doing a worksheet on the same subject; also in history or in English fiction, freeze-frame and thought-tracking methods can be used to explore character or plot, or to throw light on a situation in PSHCE. For this latter subject there's also the very effective forum theatre method, where a rehearsed or improvised performance is created, which demonstrates some kind of moral or social dilemma.

This could address issues such as bullying or any other aspect of school life where different points of view and actions need to be explored. The play is then restarted and children in the audience are asked to replace or add to the characters on stage to present their own interventions: to offer different ways of solving the problem. This works especially well because it's a space where children's voices and concerns about school life, or larger issues, are heard in public, but safely depersonalised because they are performing in role.

Equally effective instrumental uses of drama can be made when teachers or drama practitioners work with children with SEN. Programmes such as London Bubble Theatre's Speech Bubbles franchise, which works with children with speech, language or communication delay, use drama to develop communication skills. Drama facilitator Nadya Bettioui, who is currently working from a youth theatre company to deliver the year-long Speech Bubbles programme, describes her work in a Hackney primary school with Year 1 and 2 children, all of whom have speech and language delay or ADHD:

> 'There are ten children in each 45-minute weekly session, which is highly structured and consistent: a chant, a song and other activities. At the end one child stays behind to tell me an invented story. This is scribed and used for the following week's session where it is narrated by me and acted out by the children in a story square. There's a lot of facilitator guidance here: I'll be asking children to imagine what a character might say in a given situation. At the end each child confides to the programme mascot, Millie the toy cat, what they most enjoyed in the session. Whatever the children say is accepted, even if it's "the best bit was when a zombie came into the classroom and walked around". This might be the first time that that child has said anything at all.'

Progression in the Speech Bubbles programme is tracked via an online monitoring portal, with the class teacher doing a pre-assessment before the start of the programme. After every session Nadya discusses each child with the two learning support assistants. A scoring system grades the children based on the criteria of receptive, attending and expressive skills and these are followed every week after the session. The ongoing research has shown that by the end of the programme, the impact in terms of all three criteria is considerable and London Bubble are now rolling it out in a research partnership with King's College London, the Royal Society of Arts (RSA) and the Education Endowment Foundation (EEF).

In addition to the outcomes for the participating children, the medium of drama also offered incidental benefits for the learning support assistants. Both volunteers and with EAL, they reflected that they were developing their own communication skills alongside those of the children and they understood that their participation in the programme had helped them to raise their own self-esteem as professionals.

Nadya also uses drama skills in larger-scale interventions that address societal issues such as crime, by working with primary-age children in the school setting. The current Home Office 'Knife Free' initiative and the Mayor of London's 'Knife Crime Strategy' jointly fund theatre practitioners, including Nadya, to work on the theme of safe behaviour with Year 5 and 6 children in schools on local estates where knife crime is rife. The form of the workshops developed by Immediate Theatre was based on a balancing of the priorities of the funders, the schools, the needs of the children and the aims of the company who are contracted to deliver the workshops.

These are held after the schools' headteachers have approved the workshop plan, which Nadya sends them in advance. She comments that heads say that they really want to see the plan and to consult parents – it's a potentially sensitive issue because the workshops do involve discussions about knife crime – but in reality no head has ever fed back to her before the workshops, nor attended one. This is probably more of a reflection of the multiple demands on headteachers' time than of a lack of interest! But it does touch on the idea that senior leaders who are investing in arts programmes or practitioners for their schools can only benefit from a close scrutiny of the quality of the offer. Nadya does however insist that the class teacher attends the workshop in case of disclosure, and so that they can follow up where necessary. These kinds of sessions are most likely to involve disclosure because the nature of drama provides opportunities for feelings about real-life situations to rise to the surface; it's a space where, as she says, 'children open up very quickly when they are allowed to say what they think'. As for class teacher involvement, Nadya finds that some join in the sessions in a highly engaged way, while others 'sit quietly at the back of the room catching up with marking… as a former teacher I can empathise with that because they've got an hour off!' But, she adds, 'that comes from leadership and the message that's being fed back to them from their headteacher.'

Nadya describes a typical drama game played during one of the workshops, which explores the nature of safety in a community:

'It's called guardians and angels. It's usually known as prisoners and guards but I try to avoid anything too violent – there's enough of that as it is. Half the children sit in a circle of chairs (the angels) and the other half, the guardians, are standing behind them: their job is to look after the angels. There's one empty chair with a guardian behind it and that guardian has to wink at one of the angels to get them to come and sit in the empty seat. Here we're using non-verbal communications and we're also exploring the idea of what it feels like to be safe with your guardian and what happens when you take the risk to move into the empty chair – the place where you transition between being safe and unsafe. After that game we have a discussion, and already by then the children are making links with their real-life situations: "It made me feel safe like when I'm at home with my Mum and Dad and we're watching TV." They also start to connect the game with the awful things they've witnessed, which are often very shocking.

The other thing I do with my colleagues is to stand in the middle of the circle with signs saying "very risky", "risky" and "less risky". We don't want it to become too polarised: a less risky situation is on a scale; it can become more risky. We then take a few examples of situations and the children have to come and stand physically next to the sign that describes the behaviour. That's always interesting and it's a way of getting them physically involved. It's more than just putting hands up to answer. It often ends up as a debate. We're sometimes just listening to a debate between two children. The example situation might be "going to the shop with your friends after school" and most of the children would gravitate to the "less risky" sign for that one but one child might go to "risky" and say, "It depends if the shop is very far from your school." They really start to pick the issue apart and have a proper discussion. There's often one or two who are also playing devil's advocate or who try to disrupt or challenge the group by saying something like, "Being at home is very risky", but I always accept that and just ask them to explain their reasoning – and of course for some children it really might be.

Finally the adults put on a short scene illustrating one of the situations. It might be someone approaching an eight- or nine-year-old and giving them a package to look after. It's quite knife-shaped but some of them don't identify it as a knife straight away, though some really do. Then we use forum theatre to get the young people to stop the action when it's getting a bit too risky.

Drama **81**

Sometimes it takes them a long time to stop it, but we often do it a few times, and get them to think about it more deeply each time.

It's difficult because we can't shy away from the topic – even in the discussion at the beginning of the first workshop, the children are talking about knives, saying that lots of people in the neighbourhood have them, how they remember a stabbing right outside the school gates, when the children had had to be shut in the classroom for an hour afterwards. They're completely aware of it and we're here to deal with the issues, so we'll deal with them.'

Here I think about some of the small rural primary schools I have visited and understand that not all primary schools are challenged in the way that such edgy urban areas are, but every school will have concerns or preoccupations that can be usefully explored through the use of such drama techniques, either by trained class or specialist teachers or by visiting experts.

Intrinsic

Using drama skills for their contributive value in this way can also inform drama as an art form, as something of which the primary aim is intrinsic (here aesthetic), rather than instrumental. This could involve a theatrical production, perhaps of a scripted play or musical, or else of a semi-devised play, something halfway between process theatre or drama game and a fully scripted work. All can be valuable in their own ways but taking the devised route can be a way of ensuring that children's own creativity always remains a priority. Here a teacher would write an outline script and, without showing it to the children, ask them to improvise scenes based on the narrative, perhaps using some of the techniques described above to explore character or motivation more explicitly. The teacher then either notes down or records the invented dialogue and includes as much of it as meets the overall artistic imperative in the final script. In this way children's own words become part of the work of art; they hear them reflected back in rehearsal or performance and their investment in and ownership of it are consequently deeper.

In a hard-pressed school, the extra time needed for this kind of script development for the annual or termly production may not be available, but all the headteachers I have interviewed seem to agree that when they do take place, such productions are highlights of the school year. Whether as PR opportunities – the photos in the local paper or coverage on social media – or as a means of encouraging hard-to-reach families into the school, or as opportunities for teachers with musical or set-decorating talents to shine, quite apart from the performers learning dramatic skills, these events have many pay-offs, which make the heroic efforts involved on the part of staff more than worthwhile.

What makes a successful school production? We could think about scale and ambition first. As you know well, the production is probably the biggest event in the year, involving more people having to work together with a single common purpose than at other times. The commitment by staff and children to seeing something through as unwieldy and as unpredictable as a play with music is considerable, because of course the final outcome, the performance, needs to be so perfect, as perfect as possible. You have, after all, invited an audience into your space and you want and need to satisfy and delight them. There will be so many pressure points – from conflicting overlaps in different staff roles, to no-shows of children or staff, to the looming deadline of the first (or only) night, all the previous factors having shaken the director's confidence in being able to deliver the show at all. Rehearsals will be crucibles of frustration, with fluffed lines, missed cues, ill-fitting costumes, accidents on stage, children messing about on the side waiting to come on, you know that scene. But the resilience developed by the team in dealing with those setbacks, in coming back to the next rehearsal and starting again in good humour, is something everyone can witness together and be proud about. The drama skills so evident onstage, the verbal and non-verbal communication that takes place, the teamwork, and the reliance each actor has on the next one to be able to deliver his or her part are also being mirrored behind the scenes by the producers, the lighting technician or the stage manager, and by the people who have made the costumes or scenery. Everybody is totally dependent on everybody else and so the show's success also belongs to everybody.

Given this situation, it seems important to acknowledge every single role, rather than highlighting star performers. This is something that can be well expressed when a programme is produced where the credits are written in a non-hierarchical way: with an alphabetical list of every child and adult's name, with their role next to the name.

The opportunities for staff teamwork and creativity should also not be ignored. At Wootton Bassett Infants' School in Wiltshire, the head, Mark Hazzard, admits that the Christmas productions he puts on could be seen as rather teacher-led, but he believes that it is a genuinely broadening experience for the children when they are exposed to something highly professional (here in the theatrical sense of really impressive costumes, scenery and lighting). Mark writes the script, but this will be modified and the play cast by the class teachers, 'who know the children much better than I do', as he says. The costumes might be designed by a teaching assistant and the teaching assistant team will take charge of the costume production, buying the fabrics, allocating the sewing to parents and collecting the finished costumes. This is a level of responsibility that these teaching assistants don't normally enjoy and so it is especially motivating. All the class teachers too will stay behind after school to paint the scenery, something they actually relish. This is, as Mark comments, because it's the one chance they have in the year to work together as a group that is not a staff meeting or a planning session, and where the result is a joint creative work. In making art themselves, they experience that pleasurable state of concentrated physical creation that all children also deserve in the classroom and so they are more inclined to offer it.

As with most schools, the Christmas production at Wootton Bassett is also a tradition that parents want to be a part of, and not just to see their loved little ones performing, vital as that is. Mark describes how having very high production values has created a sense of anticipation for the event, which always sells out several performances. When I went along to see for myself, I sat in a packed school hall where, without any encouragement to do so, families waited in hushed silence for a full ten minutes for the show to begin. I can't say exactly what this was about, but perhaps it was a sense of being in the presence of something exceptional, something outside normal experience, and it is true that several of these families would never normally go to a theatre.

This year the show was a nativity, with a script loosely based on Michael Morpurgo's *On Angel Wings* and an accompaniment of songs. Every child in the four Year 1 and 2 classes had a role and a proper costume; the stage set featured a beautifully constructed wooden stable made by a former staff member's husband and a painted wooden backdrop of Bethlehem and the night sky, into which a parent had drilled hundreds of small holes. Fairy lights twinkled from these and, combined with the stage lights, they set up a magical experience for audience and performers alike. This is the concept of the school show using the arts – drama, visual art and music – as a vehicle for community cohesion: where the staff's pride in their creative contribution (costumes and scenery) and the children's pride in performing in front of their adults connect with the audience – the wider community outside the school. Unlike comparable events, sports days or end-of-term award ceremonies, the school show is not about winning, or at least it doesn't concern individual winners; like all theatre, it creates a shared experience where the people on the stage and the audience affect each other in an extraordinary way. All are touched by an imaginative vision brought to life by the performers and producers of the event.

Going out to drama

If there is such value in going to see a show, should that also be an integral part of a school's drama curriculum? There are obviously many shows aimed at the primary school market in theatres across the UK and, though there may be funding issues if you cannot subsidise trips for your poorest families, the experience of being in the audience for a quality show will be a richly layered and memorable one: the first time you step into a new kind of public building, sit in the plush seats and are enveloped in velvety darkness when the house lights dim, and of course the magic of what appears on the stage, as if out of nowhere. I was recently at a performance of *Macbeth*, a GCSE text for the year, sitting among many London teenagers. Their empathetic responses to the action were authentic: unsuppressed gasps of horror as Macbeth emerged in a blood soaked costume from murdering Duncan, whistles at the couple's lingering kiss. Not so different, you might imagine, from the groundlings' reaction when this play was first performed at the Globe theatre in Jacobean days. For many children, acting is being in a film, a soap opera or possibly reality TV(!) and the idea of real-life actors in your physical space is a novelty and possibly also the spark that will make them want to join the profession one day.

If going out to the theatre is impossible for financial or geographical reasons, there's always the option of inviting theatre companies into the school. We'll look at the way the Royal Shakespeare Company (RSC), among others, does this in the case study on page 86. There are advantages to this: zero transport costs and late pick-ups after school; the beauty of the everyday spaces where children feel comfortable being transformed by the presence of costumed actors and props; in the case of the RSC, the joy of having actors around the school in role, even when offstage having a coffee; and the potential to address a residual reluctance on the part of a few teachers I have come across, for whom theatre culture can occasionally still seem elitist. Teachers working in schools in the big metro cities with large BAME populations, for example, speak about 'restrictive theatre etiquette' and about how their students don't always see reflections of their own communities on the stage. So it was instructive for me to be at a performance at London's Old Vic theatre (a traditional space by any standards) of *Sylvia*, a hip-hop musical about the suffragette Sylvia Pankhurst, where virtually the whole cast was African-Caribbean, including a charismatic Delroy Atkinson as Winston Churchill. This fact was a cause of astonished delight in the young audience. As one teacher in the audience said of her Year 7 class, 'At the beginning they were all on their phones and now the phones have all gone away...'

On balance I believe that the ideal way of experiencing live theatre is to enter its imaginative world in a dedicated theatre space, with all the extra sensations that such places offer: the lights and sound effects, the anticipation of the audience, hushed or noisy, and the suspension of disbelief that the action on the stage conjures in us; that is the way that really widens opportunities for our children. A theatre trip builds cultural capital, something of immense value, both in the moment and also for the future. These kinds of encounters serve those children who will aspire to higher education at Russell Group universities, where they will be competing with their peers for whom these things are a norm; equally, though, they may spark ambition in those with fewer life chances, who, as a result of that single, exhilarating experience, might one day see a career in the creative industries as a possibility; we owe these children especially such trips.

Case study 4: Springhead Primary School, North Staffordshire

I found this school by accident on the RSC website, as it was at the time a hub school in the RSC's Learning and Performance Network. (It is now an associate lead school in a different initiative.) The Learning and Performance Network was a long-term partnership with primary, secondary and special schools, regional theatres and teachers, with an aim to: 'Bring about a significant change in the way young people experience, engage with, and take ownership of the work of Shakespeare.' (RSC, 2016) Shakespeare does of course feature in the curriculum of countless primary schools: I have watched Year 2 classes perform scenes from *A Midsummer Night's Dream* and *The Tempest*, an (abridged) *Macbeth* by a Year 5 class, and countless other successful examples of teachers introducing and presenting the stories from the plays in new, imaginative ways. From the headteacher's testimony on the website, it sounded as if this school had embraced Shakespeare in a particularly wholehearted way and, curious to learn more about how this kind of intensive focus might work, I visited the school. I soon realised that there was something different about Springhead, a smaller than average primary on an estate in the Stoke suburb of Talke Pits. Its head, Brian Anderson, comes across as a modest man but is evangelically committed to the vision of teaching and learning through Shakespeare that he developed through the RSC partnership. I wanted to know what drew him to it in the first place and, like so many of the heads I met, he brought up a personal narrative:

My wife and I always felt there were huge benefits in the arts and we got our four children involved in drama. They went to drama groups from quite a young age. One of our sons was slightly dyslexic but he did drama at GSCE and did well, and now he's doing really well doing drama at college. But we are destroying all that now. [He said this with feeling, alluding to the effective narrowing of the secondary curriculum brought about by recent education reforms. His face brightened as he continued, however.] *It's different at primary level. Ofsted seem to have changed – they're recognising the power of the arts, and the power of cross-curricular teaching, as you can see from our report. We started by connecting with the New Vic Theatre in Newcastle-under-Lyme – this was through a Creative Partnerships initiative, and later the RSC came in when the New Vic joined their network of theatres.*

The schools joining the RSC partnerships at the time signed up to objectives that included building confidence in the teaching of Shakespeare, finding new ways of bringing the work of

Drama   **87**

Shakespeare to life for young people and using the arts to bridge the transition between primary and secondary school for students. But what I witnessed in this school went much further than this. 'The breadth and quality of the curriculum at Springhead Primary shine out as major strengths' proclaimed their 2017 Ofsted report, and it was exactly how the stimulus of Shakespeare had been used in this way to make this curriculum so bright, fleet-footed, ambitious and generous, so coherently cross-curricular, that also struck me. When I visited, Julius Caesar had invaded the school. Not just the play, though that was at the centre, but through history, geography, art, craft and design, and literacy at a really high level, and it was operating throughout the school, starting with the nursery.

I watched a nursery class where the teacher was introducing the topic. On the screen was a slide of a portrait bust of a Roman emperor, and another of the Colosseum. 'This is Rome and we're going to learn about Julius Caesar,' she begins. 'What can you tell me about him?' The answers come flying: 'He's different', 'He's got different hair', 'He's got leaves'. The teacher picks up, 'Yes, he's got a crown of leaves, just like you've started to make over there in our role play corner. So this is Julius Caesar and this story is all about him; he lived in Rome and had a big, big army. Stand up and show me how you would be a soldier in Caesar's army… Oh, Alice is marching [they all start marching]. Caesar was going back from one of his great battles and all the people in Rome are really pleased because he's won the battle. Tell me, if you were one of those people what would you be doing?' 'Smiling?' comes one reply before another says, 'I would be scared 'cos he looks different.' The teacher goes on, 'The people were all very busy in Rome doing their shopping and going about their daily business.' Here the children act out a Roman shopping scene with props, terracotta jars and plates, old coins and makeshift togas.

This was an example of good Early Years teaching: I saw sparky interchanges between the children and their listening teacher, who built on their responses, and there was plenty of physical activity and meaningful, engaging role play, and so of course the children were full of concentrated enjoyment; but that half hour added up to much more than a good lesson, because it was a part of a big whole, in which learning was shared through richly extensive displays and through assemblies, performances and the live stream from Stratford. So the children in that nursery class were 'getting' Julius Caesar and Roman history in multiple ways: they were being collectively switched on to new knowledge, skills and experiences.

Brian recalled the moment when he first presented the staff with the idea of making Shakespeare the curriculum lynchpin: 'I remember the look on the face of one of the nursery teachers! But she's fine now,' he laughs. It wasn't just the teachers who were sceptical: 'We had to justify the benefits of this to the chair of governors. He wanted to know how the project would impact on children's learning. He's convinced now.' It had clearly been a challenging five-year journey to introduce and grow this new kind of curriculum, to have everyone on the staff and governing body fully signed up to it, but my conversation with the nursery teacher and the evidence from that classroom were beginning to suggest to me that it was a fruitful one.

Concentrated chatter, not silence, greeted me in a Year 5 class, where groups of children were working on different activities. There was art on one table, where Roman banners were being painted with great glee. At another the children were writing and they were keen to tell me about their engagement with Shakespeare. One of them remembered having been in *Henry V* when in Year 2. 'I was picked to act – I was a horse keeper,' she told me triumphantly. Now, having worked on Brutus's speech 'Friends, Romans, Countrymen' for their performance of the play, they were writing playscripts based on it, in which they were bringing in other characters to interrupt the speech. The class teacher Kate Condliffe explained:

The children have developed real resilience through working with Shakespeare. They go on a journey with the texts we work with. By the time we had the live stream of Julius Caesar in school, we had already looked at Brutus's speech and had started to put it in our own words and today we wanted to do something different. Tomorrow we'll be comparing it with Mark Anthony's speech. They are really showing understanding now; they're beginning to think about things that are quite meaningful and thoughtful, such as: what

Drama

might have been in that character's mind? They understand about the use of rhetoric, the use of emotion, the use of reason, the use of balanced argument; these are quite high-level skills, and now they can talk about that Brutus funeral speech eloquently.

Each child clearly did understand the task, as well as the grammar and language learning that naturally came out of it, and they did indeed talk confidently about what they were doing. 'I like Shakespeare,' one boy observed casually. 'I like the language he uses. He uses really interesting words like "loath".' Kate also remembered a girl from the term when they'd been focusing on *The Two Gentlemen of Verona* and had come across the word 'sluggardise' (meaning to make lazy). 'Two weeks later the girl came in from PE and said to the teacher, "I'm absolutely sluggardised"!'

In this context, Jacqui O'Hanlon, the RSC's Director of Education and the person magnificently responsible for the programme, describes how she sees children continually learning new words: 'Shakespeare is just a new set of really gorgeous, delicious, intriguing words [...] You ignite a curiosity about language. And that is a fantastic skillset, particularly for people from disadvantaged backgrounds.' (Turner, 2018)

This engagement with language has even been noticed by moderators such as Jan Anderson, who looks at the writing produced by Year 6 children who have been working on the Shakespeare project:

The quality of children's writing – especially when they are writing as a direct result of the rehearsal room techniques – has improved enormously and enabled more children to achieve expected and beyond by the end of key stage two. This finding was reflected in our partner schools and through my work as a moderator of writing at year six.

One of the markers of writing at greater depth is the writer's ability to make carefully considered, deliberate choices to affect the reader. I found that this was far more prevalent in writing inspired by Shakespeare's plays, which children had explored using rehearsal room techniques than in other writing. One child, writing in role as Titania, justifying her decision to keep the changeling boy in a letter to Oberon, wrote: '...a mother who died with a wish on her lips. A wish that...', thus making a deliberate choice to gradually reveal the wish to the reader in a bid to increase their interest. She went on to write: 'You cannot, shall not and never will...', deliberately using patterning with modal verbs to show the reader how adamant Titania was about her decision.

Another child writing a pair of similar letters, one from Oberon asking for the child and a reply from Titania, signed off his first letter with 'Mighty Oberon' and began his reply from Titania with 'Mighty Oberon' in quotation marks as a deliberate way of suggesting sarcasm to the reader.

I believe that it is partly due to children's realisation that Shakespeare makes such carefully considered choices, which encourages them to do the same thing; when studying the iambic pentameter rhythms in parts of Macbeth some children commented on how much time those choices must have taken to write. However, I feel that their ability to make these choices with such careful consideration of the reader is due to their increased cognitive ability to do so because, by the time they come to write, they have already made decisions and internalised much of the writing process and so they can really focus on making those higher order decisions.

The children also become very accustomed to constantly considering the effect on the reader when they use rehearsal room techniques to explore plays: we are effectively asking them to assess this whenever they do any drama work with text – making a frozen image of 'a devilish fiend' means that each child has to consider how that phrase affects their stance, expression and feelings before making that image and they then go on to see how the same phrase affected other children. They are then able to apply this skill in their writing. (Anderson, 2017)

Back to Kate's Year 5 classroom: a third group in this class were working on comic strips – a combination of art and writing skills, which works particularly well with children for whom extended writing presents a special challenge. Here, Kate pointed out another important benefit that Springhead's philosophy brought to these particular children, and to everyone else besides:

> As a teacher you have different conversations with children when the arts are taking place – especially in terms of building relationships, which is so core. When they're painting they really are free to chat and they'll tell you what they did at the weekend for example; or it might be topical things that come out of the play we're focusing on. In drama, with its physical responses, they're able to show different sides of themselves and I start to understand them better. If you're purely dealing with the head and the knowledge... you don't get the same connection; it's also a way of children seeing you as a person, what your values are and how you value their work. I found a good example of this with painting recently: in geography we were working on a piece linked to maps, using Ordnance Survey maps. The children created a linked work of art and we started to have a conversation about journeys. One girl was very fed up with what she'd done and said, 'This is rubbish! I want to start again' and I said, 'Don't start again, because you're going on a journey yourself with this picture and we don't know where you'll finish.' I'm quite tough when it comes to art – I don't just let them have another piece of paper and begin again. But by the end of the lesson this girl said, 'It's the best thing I've ever done' and I said, 'Yes, now there are layers in your work and you see where the mistakes were. And when you persist with something you've built resilience; what seemed like a mistake before now looks really good, with interesting colour combinations. That wasn't something you'd intended!' Before you know it, you're talking about some really core skills, like sticking at it, about how mistakes don't matter and that actually happy mistakes can be really effective. And then you also begin to think like an artist. This is the way professional artists work – Monet would never have said that a huge canvas was no good and he needed another one. Arts subjects really lend themselves to evaluation and critical thinking about your own work; you're developing a critical eye and mind and sharing it with the rest of the class.

The evidence is there that this approach at Springhead has results: 'With our work with the RSC we've proved that we've raised standards for literacy,' Brian says. 'Before we brought Shakespeare to the school our average points score was 3.4 and we raised it to 3.9 (since then the assessment systems have changed of course) and with our Year 6 children we find that we have never got writing out of them like this before. It's the empathy they have, the feelings about characters and situations in the plays. What schools normally do is just get children to sit down and write cold, or else they don't exploit the opportunities that are there. Teachers need to be able to say, "How can I make the most of it?" If actors come in and do a drama workshop, children need to do the writing there and then – the next day it's too late!'

We talked a bit more about the empathy and confidence that working with and through drama brings, and how it affects general behaviour. Brian remembered a particular child:

We were doing King Lear *and there was a boy in one class who did not live with his parents. The children were doing some work on the subject of family love and the teacher said, 'You always love someone. You always love a member of your family', but the boy suddenly said, 'No, my mum gave me away.' He'd never said that before. The other children asked him about it, and in that setting he had the courage to answer them. The other thing we should mention here is that the behaviour has changed completely. It's better in the playground because our drama workshops are often about problem-solving and children learn that the solution doesn't always have to be directed by an adult. In the corridors the only time you have to slow children down is first thing in the morning – they're so keen to start working! In fact behaviour is the best it has ever been in the last two to three years. I think it's partly also the way that everyone now works together – teachers with each other, children with each other and teachers with children – it's a whole philosophy.*

I asked Brian what the secret was in creating and implementing a curriculum like this. 'Flexibility' was his unhesitating answer:

When the National Curriculum was changed in 2014, there was more emphasis on English and maths but more freedom for the other non-core subjects. Many heads put in a rigid curriculum for the non-core subjects but we concentrated on skills, not knowledge, and on enjoyment in learning. When we focus on a Shakespeare play, that's the opportunity and the timetable is flexible around it. I really trust teachers with timetable. It does tend to be English and maths in the morning but that can easily change – a whole morning can be taken up with art. Things can be moved around where necessary; it's all about having that motivation. We look at the way we teach Shakespeare and ask: how can we use these approaches to impact across the curriculum? With our RSC partnership we work with other local schools; the ones who get it are the ones who are really letting teachers go with it and taking risks – teachers have to take risks. This year some of the other schools in the hub have joined just because they can see the power of this.

There is also a need to get the underpinning vision expressed clearly enough for everyone to apply it to every activity. In Springhead, the three phrases that do this all relate to skills: first, 'basic skills'. Brian says, 'You can't do anything without them. You can't research and explore without solid literacy skills, for example.' Then there are 'creative skills', which speak for themselves, and finally 'interpersonal skills' – knowing how to work together effectively. This applies to staff. As Kate says, when they put the art up around the school, there's a sense of shared work, which really unites the staff: 'You're not just in your own little room with your own curriculum – the whole school is very different when people are not locked in classes, and that feeds into the children. They see how we interact and how we value their work – how the school is transformed by their work.' This co-dependence is, as Brian points out, a great strength of the arts: 'I found out that teamwork takes place in the arts just as much as in sport. If we do a play and one child doesn't turn up they've let all the others down; it's not like that in football.' The last key word was support. Alongside encouraging the teaching staff,

Brian emphasises the need for governors to be solidly onside. He feels that this can be achieved through advocacy, certainly, but also by having governors present in school, witnessing the activity and its effects on the children. And lastly it can happen when you develop a governing body whose membership reflects the direction the school has taken. A professional from the cultural sector was recently recruited in the role of head of education at the New Vic Theatre, Newcastle-under-Lyme (the local partner organisation in the RSC project). These kinds of appointments can be of immense use in offering fellow governing body members an insider-outsider perspective on the value of arts teaching.

The other key stakeholders are of course the parents. Brian recalled that when the school first started with its Shakespeare curriculum, the parents didn't often come to performances. The reason? Because as teenagers they themselves had been bored by Shakespeare at school, or they believed it was 'for posh people'. What did work though was a sharing assembly where a drama lesson was presented. 'That was when they saw the point,' Brian explained, 'and also now all the parents value the Shakespeare project as a learning opportunity because the children are always talking about it.' The ultimate proof that parents were convinced about its value was when the school planned a theatre trip to Stratford: 'We took all of Years 4, 5 and 6, and bear in mind that we have higher than average pupil premium students; before, their parents wouldn't have paid for a trip like that, but this time they did.'

I made a second visit to the school as I wanted to see for myself how the children would react to the live RSC performance of *The Comedy of Errors*, the second of the two annual Shakespeare plays that the school covers each year; this was not, I imagined, an obviously appropriate primary school text, with its contorted plot about twins, couples and mistaken identity. But even before the start, the hall was alive with the excitement of Year 5 and 6 children from the other schools in the hub, and one Year 3 class from Springhead. The actors were already moving energetically around the set, answering the children's 'Who are you?' questions and playing a variety of instruments: drums, bass, flute, sax and guitar. By the time the play actually began, the children were fully caught up in the action, even if much of the dialogue flashed past ununderstood. A few children were given small parts, confidently performed, which was a new focus of attention. The comedy was properly played for laughs; every now and then an actor would go off-script: 'Why are you laughing?' one said to a giggling girl in the front row. 'You're not meant to laugh at Shakespeare!' Afterwards, I talked with an ecstatic group of children:

'I really liked that! It was so funny. It was humour for children! They were all laughing at certain times and I liked that!'

'I liked the expressions on the actors faces – it told the story about what happened.'

'And even when they were not acting the actors still had the expressions on their faces.'

'The one with blonde hair, she really looked as if she was going to cry...'

'I loved every moment! I loved it when Dromio slid across the floor.'

This was theatre as Shakespeare might have recognised it, with an audience participating as completely as the actors.

As I left for my train, my own thoughts sparking with the energy of this school, I noticed a large transparent geodesic dome on a grassy hill by the playground. 'We really struggle with space for practical work here,' Brian told me, 'so we've created this outside classroom. It's perfect for teachers doing drama and for children to practise in too.' This structure, mildly incongruous in its setting, seemed to me a kind of metaphor for the extraordinary Shakespeare-led curriculum Brian and his team have created at Springhead: well designed and robust, but at the same time surprising, visible, translucent and a real house for creativity.

The learning from the Springhead experience is many-layered. It's certainly an example of a headteacher who had been at a school for several years before deciding to take a bold new direction with curriculum, which could at the time have been seen as quite counter-cultural. So it's definitely a leadership story. It was also an example of the head's belief in his staff's own creative ownership of curriculum. As he says, he wants to see them doing different things every year, and to seize every opportunity for learning: the 'if it was snowing today we'd be out in that playground' approach. But, as Brian Anderson would be the first to admit, it was the stimulus of working with a strong cultural partner such as the RSC that really enabled him to do it.

The story of the RSC's education adventure is also something to think about, demonstrating as it does how a publicly funded arts organisation (23 per cent of its income came from Arts Council England grants in 2017–8) reaches out to communities well beyond its normal visitor base. It programmes Shakespeare's plays, but also those of his contemporaries, as well as new work, and its approach to production is always questioning. It aims to make the plays relevant to contemporary audiences, using Shakespeare's own inventive qualities as a springboard. As the company website says, 'We are inspired by Shakespeare; he was a daring innovator, experimenting with both form and content in his plays, so we are interested in ideas which are either radical or mischievous or both.' (RSC, 2015)

This investigative approach is carried through to its philosophy of education, which is based on the same rehearsal room techniques as those used by the RSC actors: teachers then learn these through CPD programmes based in Stratford, or, in a different model, the RSC team comes to schools. These techniques encourage young people to explore Shakespeare's words on their feet, speaking them aloud. This certainly addresses the need to get to grips with Shakespeare's language, which can ask a lot of a 21st-century audience (although as Brian points out and my own experience confirms, 'Adults want to understand every word, but with children it doesn't matter'). Ninety-four per cent of the schools participating in the RSC programme said that the work was a 'catalyst' to helping their students 'find their voice – improving pupils' language skills and confidence to use language (reading, writing, speaking)' and many connected their improved SATs results with the programme (RSC, 2018). But the techniques seem to do much more. In my conversation with Brian, the topic of empathy came up several times in terms of writing, where he felt that the Year 6 intake who had 'grown up' with the Shakespeare project were demonstrating a real ability to identify with the characters they were describing and also in the writing of playscripts when, for example, they independently devised a piece for assembly. The teacher had given them the theme of empathy and the children came up with an idea about 'belief: how different people believe different things'. This was explored at a sophisticated level, which Brian feels would not have been possible without the RSC input.

Jacqui O'Hanlon, RSC's Director of Education, also pointed out how, after ten years of close relationships with schools, there was also payback for the RSC. It was now recruiting new talent out there in the schools network, including both actors and technical staff. And because the network schools tend to be in areas of economic disadvantage, the company was also addressing the issue of diversity: it was proving that Shakespeare is not just 'for posh people'.

If in your locality there is a state-subsidised arts organisation with an education or learning department, this is the kind of work it should be doing or at least aiming for. And if it isn't, it's up to local headteachers to encourage these organisations to help provide the arts expertise that may be in short supply within the schools. At its most sustainable, this will be a long-term engagement with schools, based on CPD, as the RSC offers, so that the teachers are becoming skilled practitioners too. If it's a performing arts organisation, it needs to offer accessibly priced tickets to performances, backstage tours, meet-the-performers sessions and opportunities for children to perform in the venue in front of their parents. If this venue or company does all these things, the likelihood is that such community engagement will result in the community, the parents of the school children among them, becoming closer, buying more tickets or even just using the cafe.

Chapter 6
Literature: reading and writing it (and speaking it too!)

> *'Through reading in particular, pupils have a chance to develop culturally, emotionally, intellectually, socially and spiritually. Literature, especially, plays a key role in such development.' (Department for Education, 2014)*

Reading and writing literature, you may say to me, is an art that you have at your fingertips, one that belongs in those areas of curriculum and skills that you already cover extensively: it is highly assessed and measured; it takes place daily; teachers have been trained, re-trained and trained again to teach it; there is no need to advocate for more curriculum time for it, as there might be for the visual arts or drama or music, no need to rehearse the arguments in favour of children reading for pleasure or for information, nor for the imperative to speak or write fluently for the purposes of communication. In very many cases, schools are already using both fiction and non-fiction books as effective starting points for their version of the creative curriculum; everyone knows how many rich worlds and subjects literature can contain and link to, and schools are mostly very well-informed about the range of literature available. Instead, in this chapter we'll look at reading and writing behind the curriculum scenes, at the art and creativity in the fictional forms (stories and poetry) and what they have in common with the other arts and we'll think about what makes a really high-quality reading experience. We'll see what happens to children when they read works of poetry or fiction, and how their engagement with literature connects with the way that they write on their own. Lastly, we'll ask what a school might look like when it really values the reading and writing of literature for its own sake, beyond being a route to improving a school's data or SATs scores or even as a skill necessary for higher education and employment.

Voices

When young children are offered crayons and paper they will draw naturally, and, with time and practice, more fluently. But in most cases the same is not true of reading or writing, which they need to learn, using the basic tools of decoding, spelling, grammar and punctuation, and by developing the fine motor skills involved in manipulating a pencil or pen. They do of course have in smaller or greater measure the other necessary raw material – the spoken language – which is why the National Curriculum says that 'spoken language underpins the development of reading and writing' (Department for Education, 2014). As teachers we know this well and most of us will seize every engagement with a child as a chance to develop and refine spoken language: we'll praise a child for the use of an interesting word or positively correct a language misuse by repeating the correct version back. We'll ask a child to describe something and account for something else, and there are myriad other ways outside of the literacy session in which we'll incidentally extend vocabulary and concepts in the classroom.

In earlier chapters we talked about children finding their 'voices' through engagement with the creative arts, but here we can also think about voices more literally, both children's and teachers', when literature is read aloud or performed, in fact. We can make sure, because we timetable it, that even in Year 6 there are at least ten minutes a day when children are hearing good writing read aloud to them, by the teacher or even by children with confident reading levels (a Year 5 child reading to a Year 1 class perhaps). Research tells us that even in picture books, the vocabulary is far richer and more diverse than in the average adult-to-child conversation, where, for the sake of rapid communication, frequently occurring words appear much more often (see for example Massaro, 2015). So children are accessing literature that uses vocabulary and constructions beyond their speaking age, often beyond their reading age too. They are learning about how a narrative voice works, and they are loving it; we are offering them so much extra wealth there. In a recent TES article (Wilkinson, 2018), a secondary science teacher describes how he struggled with the silent reading period with his teenage tutor group, until he started reading aloud to them. What had previously been a listless 20 minutes in which students picked up books, flipped through them, or read a page or two before discarding one for another, turned into a period that was silent because the students were really listening to the reading adult. At the end they really were asking the 'What happens next?' question. You only have to look at the growth in popularity of audiobooks for adults to see that people go on enjoying being read to after they have stopped being children. For the teacher there can be nothing more rewarding than for a class to beg for a story session not to end, but if teachers are to make the most of this precious time, there are the obvious preconditions: to perform a book well you need to know it well, ideally like it too. You need to be a reader yourself. Then the text has to flow: apart from necessary pauses to clarify meaning or vocabulary, the reader needs to be able to dramatise the book, getting into character when reading dialogue, stopping for effect, knowing exactly at which point to finish the reading to leave the listeners wanting more.

But when we read stories to children in a class setting, we are doing much more than entertaining them or presenting them with good examples of literature in a format that doesn't require great effort or resilience – although of course those things are valuable too. Children listening to fiction together are taking part in another of those great shared experiences – the kind we have in a theatre or music venue, where we witness what's happening on stage together with other audience members and where our feelings about what we see are intensified for being communal. Children attending to a particularly dramatic reading from, say, the chapter in J.K. Rowling's *Harry Potter and the Philosopher's Stone*, where Harry, Ron, Hermione and Draco have to search for an injured unicorn at night time, in a forest full of lurking dangers, those children are for a moment experiencing a real shared and binding fear. They will be able to recall it later in the playground or on the way home; it will eventually become part of the group's collective memory of that particular school year, and the group and the school too will be stronger for that.

What literature does to you

Poetry is the other kind of text that deserves to be read aloud. Poetry is an allusive art – it suggests things rather than making them more precise, leaving us with questions rather than answers; sometimes that can be when its forms and language put up barriers of unfamiliarity. And for that reason, poetry is also elusive: like all art, it can't be tied down and there are no 'right answers' when it comes to its meaning. Poetry is close to music: it can be a rhythmic art and there the rhythm is a part of its appeal; so for all those reasons, it's more powerful when performed, as its earliest examples in the oral tradition always would have been. When you read a poem out loud you can dramatise it to tease out possible meanings, you can emphasise the rhythm, and you can savour its new kind of language. You might think that to perform poetry effectively you would need to learn it by heart, and that is something that the National Curriculum asks for. But is that specific act of learning really necessary? A poem can just as well be read out expressively as memorised. Children's abilities in this field are naturally so varied: one child who likes a particular poem will absorb it spontaneously without effort; another might be just as keen but without that kind of recall. Here I would recommend going to Michael Rosen (2016), the poetry king, to see what he has to say about poetry learning techniques:

> 'The best way to do it is first to read it over and over again. Second, try saying it with the poem covered up. Every time you get stuck, have a look at where you went wrong, then cover the poem again and carry on. When you get to the end, start again.'

Many schools invite poets such as Michael Rosen to visit the school to perform their own poetry. This can be exactly the thing to get children going on the writing, which we'll come to on page 110.

Poetry recitals are the public face of the form but we shouldn't leave out poetry in the private sphere. Many of the people I interviewed for this book had exceptional memories of poems read at primary school; they could either recite one or two perfectly, or at least remember a few lines. Without exception, they mentioned them as significant literary experiences – and all of them thought that this was because the works seemed to address them so personally at the time. Here are three examples, with the readers' explanations of their attraction:

Bed in Summer
Robert Louis Stevenson

In winter I get up at night
And dress by yellow candle-light.
In summer, quite the other way,
I have to go to bed by day.

I have to go to bed and see
The birds still hopping on the tree,
Or hear the grown-up people's feet
Still going past me in the street.

And does it not seem hard to you,
When all the sky is clear and blue,
And I should like so much to play,
To have to go to bed by day?

Mark (now a writer) remembers 'Bed in Summer' from *A Child's Garden of Verses*, seeing in it a perfect reflection of his own experience as a five-year-old: the irony of being made to go to bed with the sky still light but, unable to sleep, having to read his book under the dark of the bedcovers in case his mother came in.

Diane mentioned the first verse from William Blake's (1794) 'A Poison Tree', at first slightly scrambling it, but then, with much delight, recalling it word perfect:

A Poison Tree
William Blake

I was angry with my friend:
I told my wrath, my wrath did end.
I was angry with my foe:
I told it not, my wrath did grow.

And I watered it in fears,
Night and morning with my tears;
And I sunned it with smiles,
And with soft deceitful wiles.

And it grew both day and night,
Till it bore an apple bright;
And my foe beheld it shine,
And he knew that it was mine.

And into my garden stole
When the night had veil'd the pole:
In the morning glad I see
My foe outstretch'd beneath the tree.

This poem spoke to Diane at a time when, entering adolescence, her friendships and the rupturing of friendships were of consuming importance to her; being given permission by a poem to speak your anger at someone was a significant life-learning moment.

For me, it was 'Overheard on a Saltmarsh' by Harold Monro (1914).

Overheard on a Saltmarsh
Harold Monro

Nymph, nymph, what are your beads?

Green glass, goblin. Why do you stare at them?

Give them me.

No.

Give them me. Give them me.

No.
Then I will howl all night in the reeds,
Lie in the mud and howl for them.

Goblin, why do you love them so?

They are better than stars or water,
Better than voices of winds that sing,
Better than any man's fair daughter,

Your green glass beads on a silver ring.

Hush I stole them out of the moon.

Give me your beads, I desire them.

No.

*I will howl in a deep lagoon
For your green glass beads, I love them so.
Give them me. Give them.*

No.

This wonderful fairytale argument works really well in performance, by two children or two groups, but for me as a six-year-old reading it to myself, it was firstly a visual thing. Without the help of illustrations I saw those green glass beads glistening on a silver ring – I can still remember the exact shade of green. The unfamiliar layout on the page affected me too, with those potent single word lines (you could go on saying 'No' like that). A new feeling was added to my small repertoire: the sort of desire that makes you howl all night for something.

In all of these examples, the child 'owned' the poem because he or she identified with an aspect of it so completely. As one of my interviewees said, 'I thought it had been written about me.' In a few lines in poetry, or in many lines in a novel, the art of literature makes a connection between a small person's own experience and the wider world.

The challenges and consolations

Whether it's poetry or fiction, all teachers know then that reading to classes can light the fire and can inspire children to want to read for themselves – either the same book, or others by the same author. For children who have taken off on the reading flight, it's like wanting more chocolate; the pleasure is irresistible. But here I'd like to think a bit more about what motivates children to want to read by spending a bit of time in the company of those who don't: children who, despite the best efforts of teachers and many literacy strategies, still struggle with the skill, children who may eventually reach the required standard but never do find the pleasure, let alone find themselves unable to resist it. For this I went to the work of Daniel Pennac, the successful French author who was originally one of these children too, a 'dunce' as he quaintly describes himself. Pennac has written two autobiographical books on the theme of children who struggle with school learning. In *Chagrin d'école* (translated as *School Blues*), he first explains his own difficulties with both reading and writing and then the factors that eventually led him to become a school success, and later a teacher. He describes how, because of his own experience, he was able to relate to the young people who arrived in his classes with similar difficulties, and how he developed strategies for helping them. The books do relate specifically to France's very academic and monocultural curriculum and hierarchical attitude to literature, but I think they still have something to say to us about what might be going on in the learning reader's head. Here, Pennac is being interviewed about *School Blues* and gives us a child's view of the challenges:

> '*My brother used to say I had a dreadful fear of capital letters because they come before a proper noun: the name of a country, a historical personality; these [were words that] carried knowledge. A capital was... a letter that said: "Stop! This word means no entry to little idiots like you. It says... watch out! This word is going to open up all the grammar and spelling traps into which you are going to fall."*' (English PEN, 2010, translation edited by author)

Pennac really understands the humiliation of knowing how much you don't know, especially when you see your peers striding ahead; he visualises exactly how a bit of text can seem a terrifying monolith of letters and words, conspiring to prevent you ever decoding them. When I was teaching, it was sometimes the illustrations in a book that could conquer the unease felt by such a struggling reader. I was once working with a Year 3 boy who had a speech impairment that made phonics seem especially impenetrable to him, but we started on an old reading series called *Monster* by Ellen Blance and Ann Cook, illustrated by Quentin Blake. The monster in question was unfamiliar with the human world, wanted to join in, but was often hopeless or clueless at the simplest of tasks. There was something about Blake's imagining of this ungainly, heavy-footed purple creature that reassured this little boy and told him that he wasn't the only one in difficulty. It was this one character that made him really want to decode the story for himself and then to read all the rest of the series. Pennac is also good on the ways to generate enthusiasm about reading, which can trump the fear and pain that some children experience. He talks about the human body reading:

> 'At home I had mostly watched other people read: my father in his armchair... legs crossed, a book open on his knees; Bernard [his brother], in our bedroom, curled up on his side, right hand propping up his head... a sense of well-being was implied by these poses. It was the reader's physicality that got me into reading. Perhaps in the beginning, I only read in order to reproduce those postures and to explore others. And as I read I would settle down into a state of physical happiness that persists to this day.'
> (Pennac, 2007)

The idea of the joy of reading being 'caught' by the argument of another person's body rather than by their words is an attractive one to me. It made me appreciate even more the rooms I have seen in schools where proper attention has been paid to the design of places where children can read in exactly these characterful and individual ways. I have seen many schools where comfortable reading corners have all but disappeared, but at Feversham Primary Academy, for example, there was a 'soft' reading space with low lighting (not too low), carpets in warm colours, and beanbags and other seating that moulded itself to a child's body, so there was a sense of the child taking control of the activity rather than the reverse. Wootton Bassett Infants' School has recently built a new library, a 'house in the trees', a sort of wonky cottage on stilts, which, as you climb its wooden staircase, makes your heart beat with the same feelings of anticipation and delight that a good book does. Even more wondrous for a six-year-old will be the treetop walk, which will eventually link the library to another school building. This architecture communicates a sense of unbounded adventure, echoed in the external balcony spaces and the picture windows, both of which look out over the extensive Wiltshire countryside. A quick check online will show you many other examples of this kind of inviting reading environment. It's saying books really do set your mind free.

Pennac's other school-related book, *The Rights of the Reader* (2006), is well known mainly because of its accompanying bestselling poster. Illustrated by Quentin Blake in a suitably subversive way, the 'rights' include:

'**1** *The right not to read.*
2 *The right to skip.*
3 *The right not to finish a book.*
4 *The right to read it again.*
5 *The right to read anything.*
6 *The right to mistake a book for real life.*
7 *The right to read anywhere.*
8 *The right to dip in.*
9 *The right to read out loud.*
10 *The right to be quiet.*'

At the bottom, Quentin has scrawled the message: '10 rights and 1 warning: don't make fun of people who don't read or they never will!' Quentin is very well qualified to say this – when doing military service (obligatory for men until the 1960s), he was placed in the Army Education Corps, where he taught reading skills to the many young recruits who were still leaving school illiterate.

These rights and their accompanying illustrations have more than a whiff of the wonky treetop library about them – they imagine a world where, far removed from fronted adverbials, prescribed texts and endless analysis, a reader can have a personal relationship with a book. Like your relationships with trusted friends, they're not always the same: meeting a mate in a bar is different from seeing them at work, just as reading on the grass is nothing like reading at a desk; dipping into a book instead of reading it chronologically is like a short phone call as opposed to an hour's conversation over Skype. Both versions can still satisfy and on some days you might not feel like meeting up or reading your book at all.

Pennac's own early reading history is relevant. As a young reader, he started with Hans Christian Andersen's fairy tales because he 'identified with the Ugly Duckling' (Pennac, 2006), but his academic secondary school considered the reading of novels, other than set texts, as a waste of time, so at that time his book choices depended on their not being on the syllabus.

> 'Nobody could quiz me about them. Nobody could read them over my shoulder; we kept our own company, the authors and I... I read like Emma Bovary... purely to satisfy my cravings, which, luckily, proved insatiable.' (Pennac, 2007)

So there is something here about the importance of children also making their own reading discoveries in parallel to, or even quite apart from, the advice and recommendations they might get at school. But for the many children whose families do not read and for the very young, access to books outside school might be a remote luxury. A public library (if there still is one locally…), an actual or online bookshop, or a friend's house may just not be choices. This is why the school visit to the public libraries that do still exist remains such a vital one. A library, the place where, relatively free of interfering adults, a jacket illustration, a word in the title, the size or format of a book, any or all of these things, could beckon to you, and it's this kind of choosing, this feeling that a book is addressing you personally, that gives children such ownership of their reading. And the opposite of this is important too: Pennac's right of a reader *not* to finish a book, or not to start one in the first place if it doesn't seem to have much to say to you – something much trickier at school if it's a text everyone has to read, but easily done with a library book.

None of this is to deny the equally important role of schools and teachers as reading counsellors and advocates, and many have of course found original and engaging ways to generate excitement and discussion about good literature and reading in general. At The Round House Primary Academy in St Neots, for example, they have a scheme called '100 books you must read before you leave', in which the selected books are imaginatively displayed throughout the school, in a graded order, but linked by a coloured ribbon that invites you on to consider the next one. Other common measures include children's book reviews displayed in corridors or on the school website, making special displays of favourite books that children bring in from home, inviting authors to present their work to children, or celebrating World Book Day in a way that is about more than dressing up. Rachel Lopiccolo (2018), a teacher at Waddington and West Bradford CE Primary School in Lancashire, recommends:

> 'Children can dress up but, more importantly, ask them to come "in role" as their character. They could then work in groups, chatting as those characters, or even create a short drama to perform at an end-of-day assembly for the rest of the school.'

The idea of a whole school as a reading community can be a powerful one. Children who see the adults in their school (especially their favourite ones) as readers for pleasure are more likely to be convinced that they could join in too. I have seen wonderful book-sharing assemblies where both teaching and non-teaching staff have alternated with children, talking enthusiastically about the books they are reading.

Reading has to be taught to most children who arrive at school as four- or five-year-olds and its skills developed throughout primary school – no one can argue with that – but to end this reading section, let's go back to Daniel Pennac. The big underlying point and counsel of perfection in both his heartfelt books about school education is that, as far as the current system allows, our paramount concern as educators should be to ensure that all children who pass through our classrooms become people who have experienced the joy waiting inside a book, because they found one that spoke to them – whether this happened when they listened to a book being read to them in class, in a car or on a device, where they heard magical new sequences of words that wove extraordinary visions in their heads, or whether it was when they read a book to themselves in silent, page-turning delight. And, importantly, they should *never, never* be put off books because of something that happened at school.

Writing

Every time a child reads a fiction book or poem, a vista is opened of a new world beyond home and school; she is touched by different feelings, meets unfamiliar characters and situations, all voiced in a wealth of language, which she will internalise and then ideally draw on when she comes to express herself in her own writing. So reading books will be one major investment for her; the other is the framework, the spelling and grammar, the punctuation, the different styles that she has to absorb – of course she can't manage without those. But this last section is about the third element, the content, the what to write, rather than the how. When we present a child with a blank piece of paper and ask him to produce a piece of creative written work on a given subject, how can we best help him to want to put down his thoughts? Are there ways of making writing as exciting and compelling as reading can be?

A school where the arts are richly present has many ways of answering these questions. As we've seen, children who regularly participate in dance and drama, who see the work of visual artists all around them in inspiring displays or installations, are already imagining themselves into those other situations that will provide them with the writing resource. Look at a child using that picture of Phineas and his followers (see Chapter 1, page 26) as a stimulus for narrative writing: the subject may be outside his own direct experience (a banquet, soldiers in classical armour, a head with snakes and magical powers) but the way that the artist has painted it (large format, brightly coloured, with a strong sense of movement included in the brushstrokes) helps him to grasp something, to be excited and to ask more questions. If he is asked to write now, he will have the visual data to prompt him and I guarantee you he will want to put something down. A soundless animation or a textless picture book could achieve the same thing and so could music – a more abstract source, yes, but when children listen to a well-chosen and short piece of music (one of the BBC Ten Pieces, for example; see page 49), they find words not normally in their heads to express the different feelings evoked by the music. These can then be used in poetry or as the basis of a narrative – we'll see a similar idea in the case study on page 112.

Creative language is also wonderfully and differently summoned through outdoor experiences: an organisation called Cambridge Curiosity and Imagination (CCI) has developed adventurous projects with schools and their communities, based on imaginative exploration of local environments. When I visited The Round House Primary Academy in St Neots, I was led by a breathlessly excited group of Year 5 children on a tour of the local Auntie's Wood, an ordinary woodland site five minutes' walk from the school but, through the project, transformed in children's minds into a thrilling place, a site of mythical narratives. A parent of children who had taken part in a similar CCI event commented, 'My children accelerate alarmingly as we approach entrances to woods. They are happiest playing among trees. They spin fabulous stories about bizarre forest inhabitants… I love to watch as nature lights their fires.' Several publications record these nature-inspired words, including '37 Shadows: Listening to children's stories from the woods', a record of the Histon Children's Centre Footprints project, which you can find here: www.cambridgecandi.org.uk/projects/footprints/37shadows. Children's words also appear on the CCI Fantastical Maps model, where an illustrator, here Elena Arévalo Melville (see Illustration 6.1), uses them as part of a map record of each exploration; it is a sort of magical composite based on maps children have made themselves, layered with her own work. At Offord Primary School, also in St Neots, where the children had also been map-making, a class teacher told me, 'Even lower-ability children are desperate to write on their map because it means something to them.'

We all want our children to have these kinds of experiences of writing, rather than the one described by author Vanessa Harbour (2018) in this tweet about her grandson:

> 'Feeling distraught 7yo grandson having love of writing battered out of him by school. Used to loved writing stories. Now too worried he might start a sentence with the wrong word [...] had to miss assembly as was struggling to write.'

But this book is an encouragement and not a polemic, so, in the case study for this chapter, let's see another way of calling up creativity in the child-who-is-also-a-writer. We'll look at how a writer of literature helps children to look inside for inspiration…

> **Case study 5:** Grafton Primary School, Islington, London
>
> 'Writer-in-Residence' is how Diane Samuels is described at Grafton Primary, but, as well as being a trained teacher, in the rest of her life she is a successful author and playwright. Her play *Kindertransport* (Samuels, 2008) continues to be programmed around the world and is on the GCSE drama syllabus, and she teaches creative, writing at higher education level as well as in private groups. Part of the school's strong team of freelance creatives, who all practise successfully in their fields, she works with groups of children from Years 3, 4 and 5. Described as more able and talented (MAT) or able (A), MAT children have half a day with her for a term in each year and the A children half a day for half a term, and so by the end of Year 5, Diane knows the children very well, sometimes better than their class teachers do at the beginning of a new school year. Based on this kind of knowledge, real progress can be made and tracked by the year-end. But here, on a cold day in March, she is working with nine Year 3 MAT children and it's their first session as a group with her, although she has already visited the whole class to model the

teaching with the class teacher. The term's cross-curricular theme is the Stone Age and Diane has decided on 'caves' as the springing point for the lesson. The objective is to teach children writing skills, which will help them to find their own authorial voice; they will soon be discovering a new way of working.

The children arrive in a classroom (not their own) from the playground, in noisy enjoyment at being the small, select group, but Diane soon creates purposeful order by handing out new workbooks:

DS: You can decorate the cover and make it your own. Write your name in beautiful letters; write clearly and big, because it's for other people to read. You'll get used to doing things differently when you're working with me – there are no lines in these books...

Grace: Why?

DS: So you can be more creative; you can write bigger or sideways across the page. A writer has a notebook – you don't need to worry about whether it's right or correct – but you need to be able to read it and not waste paper. [Shows children her own notebook.] *I circle things, I do things sideways. You're free to explore, experiment, play, not even think. Do lots of writing and try things out.*

Amina: Can we write in spirals?

DS: Yes. Start with the cover – you can work with all four covers if you like...[DS then brings out a book of cave paintings and shows it to the children.] *Your book could look like this; it could be like the inside of a cave.*

Lucy: Cave paintings were originally black and went blue in time.

DS: Yes, I'd say you might draw creatures – they could be spirit creatures and you could wake them up. Draw from your imaginations. You can do shapes and patterns as well as creatures.

You could use different colours. It's your book and you must do it your way. What are your ideas?

Amina: *A woolly mammoth.*

Logan: *A T-Rex or a pterodactyl or a caveman.*

Mason: *An antelope or a woolly mammoth.*

Munira: *A hamster?*

DS: *That might be a first! I don't know if there's ever been a cave painting of a hamster.*

Lucy: *A tiger.*

Mia: *I might draw a chicken or a dog or a guinea pig.*

Grace: *A unicorn or a cat or a dolphin.*

Bushra: *I don't know.* [Thinks for a long time.] *A squirrel or a monkey.* [Two of the girls snigger at her.]

[Five minutes later] *A pony!*

DS: *Once you start drawing, other things might come to mind. You might all have given each other ideas. Find a quiet place in the room. You're on your own now; this is solo work, and you need to be quiet. You can write symbols, shapes or letters. As you draw you might want to share with others, but I want you to share only with yourself. Ask yourselves questions, rather than asking me.*

[The children sit at different tables. Outside it starts to snow. Mia draws snowflakes. DS comments: 'The children want to share their work, but not sharing extends and challenges them.' Mason keeps wanting to show his work to others in the class and looks for approval.]

DS: *Ask yourself if it's good. You're the expert on yourself.*

Grace: *I've finished.*

DS: *I want you to add one thing to what you've done – go beyond the point where you think you've finished…*

[30 minutes into the class and all the children are 'in the zone'.]

DS: Now open up your book and write the date. It's always worth dating things because then you know when you did something. You can write the date wherever you like.

Logan: I don't want to share my work.

DS: Why not?

Logan: It's embarrassing.

DS: What makes it embarrassing?

Logan: I'm not a good drawer.

DS: This isn't about being bad or good – it's about what we're coming up with. I write every day and I always feel a bit embarrassed, but I don't let it stop me. I think we feel embarrassed because we think we're going to be judged... but I'm curious. We could just say, 'Oh look, that's how it's turned out', so let's drop good and bad and say instead, 'The drawings are going to be what they are... be curious about them.'

Bushra: I wrote Monday instead of Tuesday.

DS: Put brackets round the word and write Tuesday. I don't want anything rubbed out or crossed out in these books. Now let's see what everyone has drawn; show us your book and tell us what you've drawn and then give me a word, any word that comes into your head and we're all going to write down that word.

Munira: I've done a giant hamster and on the back I've written the word 'Turkiye' (because I'm from Turkey) and this is myself as a llama because I like llamas.

DS: What word would you like everyone to write down?

Munira: Izmir.

Maryam: When I did my name, the A has a body, and I drew fire and snow, a no-entry sign, a big snowflake and a cup of

Literature: reading and writing it (and speaking it too!)   115 water, a golden dragon, a dream tree house and a weird spiky thing. My word is pineapple.

DS: Thank you, that was very rich.

Logan: This is a big cake that has twirly things around it; this is a big version of my name and I tried to write spaghetti. I tried to do a chameleon and it didn't work out – it's a millipede now...

DS: That's a really good lesson: when we start to write or draw and it turns into something else it shows you're alive!

Logan: I've done a couple of numbers, a potato, an egg with numbers in it, a tree, a spider and a twirly thing... everything I like in the wrong order.

DS: You're really alive!

Logan: And my word is cake.

Amina: Do I have to say anything? It's the Stone Age: blood, a woolly mammoth, that's a cliff and my word is 'sabretoothed cat'.

Lucy: This is my name in monster form, and a cave with tunnels going through it, a dragon and at the back by the cat, a melon, and here are all the seasons.

DS: In the Stone Age people were very connected to the elements.

Lucy: And my word is monster.

DS: You're all giving each other little jewels which we're going to work with. We move between sharing and going back into ourselves.

Mia: My dots are all joined together – I see lots of shapes in the dots.

Maryam [interrupts]: Everyone who can draw can write!

Mia: Inside I did the window and snow and one person looking out *at the snow. People are having a snow fight. And my word is snow.*

DS: You're making patterns with the words there – with the word 'snow'.

[Logan eventually shows mammoth.]

DS: You're not so embarrassed now!

Mason: I've done monsters, characters of descendants, a smiley face, a mammoth and an emoji, a big ladybug and my word is party.

Grace: Mine is a fish, a bee, a face, an imaginary animal, my name with a smiley face, the seasons, a computer with a hot dog app, a potato app, a food app and my word is hot dog.

Bushra: I've done my name, different colours, smiles and faces, my name again, bigger, green patterns and my word is girl.

DS: Now I'm going to give you a few words: dark, light, afraid, brave. Now you're going to make something with the words. Include all the words in any order. It doesn't need to make sense; you can make words do anything: it's called collage writing.

Logan: I can't use all those words.

DS: I believe in you. Try.

Lucy: Could I use two words together in the same sentence like 'light is dark'?

DS: Yes. Now, the start phrase is 'in the cave'. Keep it moving; don't think, just write. Use words more than once. See what can happen if you use a word more than once.

[The atmosphere in the room is now very calm, and the children write willingly, concentratedly and silently for 15 minutes until the buzzer sounds.]

We can unpick this lesson to see how and why Diane introduced the technique of collage writing. As she told the children, they would be working differently with her. To start the session she doesn't *ask* them for information, either about the Stone Age or about writing; she doesn't *tell* them, 'Today we're going to be doing some collage writing and this is how it works', but instead she *gives* them something: a workbook and pencil, the writer's tools. A gift that makes you feel chosen. And this workbook will not resemble those you are used to writing in back in your classroom: there are no lines or margins to keep you straight in this book; you're allowed to write in a direction of your choosing. There is one stipulation for the cover though and that's that your name needs to be written on it in big, beautiful, clear letters, because this book is going to be for someone else to read. Two ideas already emerge strongly about the craft of writing: first, that you are the person writing, the whole of you, not the child in class obeying other people's rules about grammar, paragraphs and vocabulary. Your name is in large letters and you can try out ideas that come from somewhere deep inside you, that make you want to write in a spiral or a square or upside down. The second thought is that writers need to consider readers, the people for whom they write, who, for example, deserve not to struggle to decode a careless script.

These gifts, which the child writers now hold in their hands, are now to become more 'their own' by being decorated or illustrated. Diane suggests that they can personalise their books and at the same time connect to the theme of caves and cave paintings, by drawing creatures of their choice. So although this is a writing session, it begins with drawing, for most children a more immediate form of expression. But at the same time, Diane asks them to come up with a single word when they make these drawings. In the initial brainstorm, some children clearly use the ideas and vocabulary associated with their topic – woolly mammoth, sabretooth tiger, caveman – but soon others are beginning to free-associate, bringing in ideas from their own home or imaginative spheres, such as hamster or unicorn, and this happens increasingly in the drawing session. Mia starts to draw what's on her mind as she gazes out of the window at the snow in the playground, and Munira portrays herself as a llama (a favourite animal) and stamps the back cover with the name of her country, Turkey, but written in the Turkish spelling, so even more personal. The children have started to loosen up: Logan, who is pessimistic about his drawing, attempts a chameleon but accepts its transformation into a millipede, while Maryam saw that the A in her name seemed to have a body, and she makes a 'dream tree house'; now the process has connected them to the creative realm. The combination of sharing ideas so that they can be aired, acknowledged and appreciated, and having quiet private space where your own ideas can surface uninterrupted, is turning out to be a fruitful one.

When they start on their final write, the children seem confident in this new way of doing things and they continue in the playful spirit: one child amusing herself by writing a word backwards and reading it out loud, another making certain words stand out on the page by writing them in a larger script. The children connect the disparate words the group has come up with in lively narratives or more fragmented text. They have learnt the technique of collage writing, producing a 'patchwork composition' where the reader experiences what you have to say rather than being given an explanation of it. Academic Peter Elbow (1998) explains:

A collage consists not of a single perfectly connected train of explicit thinking or narrative but rather of fragments: arranged how shall we say?—poetically? intuitively? randomly? Without transitions or connectives [...] When it works it is terrific. Indeed, there is often a deeper impact on readers because the collage invites them to create actively out of their own consciousness the vision which organizes those fragments—the sparks which cross those gaps.

For the Grafton children, this process has a tangible outcome: in a later session they will work on turning their piece of free writing into a new form, a poem or a prose poem perhaps. To produce this they will learn to revise and edit their work, to write it up on the computer and to think about layout and design in order to make it ready for its eventual 'publication'. Spelling and grammar will of course be involved at this stage. The writer-teacher in this school has given these children an exceptional opportunity. She shares her professional expertise generously, teaching the class in the same way as she would her adult groups; their editing, revising and layout skills are useful and transferable to writing in other curriculum areas, as are the pointers to how to write for readers. The most significant lesson, though, seemed to be the one about creativity: the one about finding your own voice (in this case your writing voice but it could have been your dance body or your artist's 'handwriting'), by connecting with your deep self. When you alternate a lively sharing of ideas with time spent in a quiet receptive state, where what psychologists call 'flow' can take place, the spark that Peter Elbow refers to above can be released, first in the writer and then later in the reader.

With these children in playful mode, we are back where we started, with our even younger children playing imaginatively. Of course, I am aware that this kind of writing session is a special one, that your whole school day will not be, cannot be like this – that you may not have such specialists on your staff, or teachers who are trained and confident in this kind of teaching approach. But this book is a plea to you as a school leader, for you to think about making space in your curriculum for these kinds of experiences, as all the leaders in the schools described here have done with great determination. None of these headteachers transformed their curriculum overnight. In almost all cases it was a slow-burning – though always strategic and purposeful – adventure, based on a recognition that numeracy and literacy can also remain, as one head expressed it, 'never far away', but balanced and always enhanced by the arts subjects. Often, as in the case of Grafton and Cleveland Road, it was a head's vision combined with really successful recruitment of the person on the team who would lead the change. Sometimes, as with Barcombe, it was the enthusiasms of one person, a TA to whom the head entrusted the blossoming of visual art throughout the school. At Feversham, it was an acknowledgement by the head that the school he had taken over was failing because the overwhelming emphasis on literacy and numeracy in the curriculum was dominating the learning agenda in a counterproductive way. And so the children were being failed by it.

But once these schools had embarked on the arts journey, there was no turning back. From the invitation to arts professionals from the wider school community to visit, to partnerships with excellent arts organisations, to the employment of specialists (whether freelance or through franchised companies) and the upskilling of teachers through CPD, to the appointing of arts governors, to the full-scale rewriting of the curriculum, as Cleveland Road did, a colourful new life has been breathed into these schools. Attendance and behaviour have improved, parents have become more closely engaged, and most of all, the children are happy because learning through the arts always addresses them personally, values them personally, affirms and expresses them, and teaches them about themselves. Who could need more than that?

Afterword

The world in miniature – Windmill Hill Primary School

This is a story about a school that no longer exists. It was the victim of a cross-borough rationalisation of sites but it stays in the memory of the people who worked and learned there because of the work of one teacher. It remains in my memory because, at a time when I had left classroom teaching for a career in the art gallery, it reminded me that the arts in the classroom have a uniquely transformative power.

One dark winter Friday afternoon when I was still working at The National Gallery's education department, my phone rang. It was late and I had almost decided to let it go to voicemail but something made me pick it up. 'I hope I'm not wasting your time,' said a voice. The man on the other end was a headteacher, David Messenger, who told me that his deputy had attended one of our training days and had done some really interesting work based on one of our paintings, the so-called Wilton Diptych (Illustration 7.1), as a result (a diptych is a foldable work in two flat sections joined by a hinge). He wondered whether I'd like to – no, his actual words were he 'thought I ought to' – come and see it. Although I dealt with teachers and their students every day, going out to see schools was not in my job description. What we offered at the time was a one-way process: an education service consisting of tailor-made gallery tours, training days and conferences for teachers, who took up this offer in great numbers. In those days (early 2000s) we had around 20 schools visiting every day and we filled our lecture theatre with 300 heads for the conference and with many more teachers over who came to the seven or so training days annually. But apart from nice thank you letters and drawings sent by teachers from their classes, I didn't have much sense of how or whether the visits were followed up back at school. David's call made me curious and the following week I took a train to Swindon. I had no idea what to expect – David had been very non-specific – but as I walked into Mark Hazzard's Year 6 classroom I stopped on the threshold.

A life-size reproduction of the painting was prominently displayed: it's a small jewel of a medieval work, about 50 x 30 centimetres in dimensions, painted on two hinged wooden panels, which show King Richard II of England with saints and the blue-robed Virgin Mary holding the baby among a group of angels, also dressed in intense blue. In some miraculous way, the picture seemed to have breathed its life all over the room. The many large display boards were covered in deep purple-blue with titles of stylish, cut-out gold italic lettering: 'History', 'Religion', 'Techniques' (see Illustrations 7.2 and 7.3). The display was a singing combination of children's work – writing, drawings, paintings – interspersed with reproductions of other images of medieval history and life. All over on the flat surfaces glinted exquisite little objects – children's own miniature versions of diptychs or triptychs painted onto wooden panels (which they had cut themselves using the class jigsaw), with proper gilded backgrounds, each different from the next in shape and imagery. I remember the word 'finish' coming into my mind. Every element, from the triple mounting, to the choice of images, to the design of each board, to the handwritten work, had been executed in loving (and that word really applied) and perfect detail. In this connection I also need to confess that, while in mid-marvelling, I had a simultaneous moment of hesitation: my own arts teaching style had been very different, based much more on children's free creative responses to stimuli, on large-scale painting and sculpture, for example, and in some ways this work seemed the opposite of that; it was teacher-led and highly contained. But then I tried to imagine myself as a ten-year-old having access to this kind of learning and production, and being surrounded by such a visual feast every day, and I accepted that there are many ways of making the arts available to children, and many ways of offering them learning through it.

Back to the room: although the work made such an impression, I was hardly aware of the teacher. He was somewhere in a corner helping a child while the rest of the class were busily writing or painting. When we eventually had time to talk, I learned that Mark had been so personally inspired by his session at the National Gallery when we had focused on the Diptych that he had planned a whole term's work around it – in fact the children were spending every afternoon with the Wilton Diptych. It was a very skills-based project: the children learned how to use a jigsaw, how to gild, and how to mix and use egg tempera paint (the medium that the medieval artist would have used – a mixture of pigment, egg yolk and water). There was also historical enquiry: Mark didn't tell the children the identity of the king and they had to discover it through researching the visual clues that the artist included, in particular the white hart (or stag), which was Richard's personal emblem. But there was knowledge too: a literary connection via Shakespeare's *Richard II*, and a religious education element dealing with angels (which appear in several world religions). I chatted with the children, who told me enthusiastically about the reign of Richard II, demonstrated gilding to me and proudly showed me their miniatures, explaining their choice of imagery. Their engagement was striking and genuine.

I left the school determined that more people should see work like this and proposed it as an exhibition at the National Gallery. The Gallery and its visitors needed to know how its collection could affect people and what it could inspire in teachers and children. To my surprise it was accepted: although the Gallery did occasionally give wall space to a staff art show, work by children had never previously been exhibited there. But this exhibition turned out to be the beginning of the Take One Picture scheme, and since then the Gallery has really bought into the scheme and the work of many thousands of children has been seen there.

I visited Windmill Hill several times before it closed in 2007. On each occasion, Mark's classroom had been transformed by the subject of the term's enquiry, which might be familiar curriculum content, such as Roman Britain, or a local building study; another time it was a landscape feature, such as the Uffington White Horse; Brownsea Island was also a geography focus one term and then the First World War came up in history. The next year a work of fiction such as *The Sword in the Stone* took over the class. Every time, the walls and flat surfaces had been rethought: alongside the children's work, honoured by the care with which it was mounted and hung, the displays were also animated by objects. The offer for the First World War included some barbed wire (well above eye-level), photos of soldiers picked up from car boot sales, a gas mask, bits of uniform and, most poignantly, miniature sections of a trench, one made by each child, with tiny mugs and miniscule grey blankets. On another visit they had focused on *The Fighting Temeraire*, Turner's celebrated and fanciful imagining of this warship, which, after her brave show at the Battle of Trafalgar, was towed along the Thames to be finally broken up. This time, a role play area had been created, a little cabin with a desk and ship's lantern and a bowl of ship's biscuits. The children had also each made and painted a small clay model of one of the Temeraire's sailors, each with an identity, which had, Mark said, inspired a special kind of empathy. When, as part of the English curriculum, the class was working on letter-writing skills, the children would beg Mark to be allowed to go into the 'cabin' and write letters home to their mothers from their little sailor avatars, stuck in such trying conditions, so far from land. Creating these characters had allowed the children to enter the space imaginatively – there was no stopping them with the writing then.

These little worlds made me think a lot about the value of the small. When I worked at the National Gallery there was at the entrance a donations box in the form of a detailed, small-scale model of the Gallery; watching people of all ages flock round it, we often thought that they showed more interest in this model than in many of the paintings inside the real thing. There's something about the miniature that we all love, not just children. Perhaps that's because we remember that when as children we played with little things, we were in control; we could see the whole rather than a detail, and so understood it better. Even more than that, when a child makes a small thing with her hands, she is also its powerful creator and this has special significance to small people at school, who so rarely occupy that position. The aim of this book has been to show that being in control of the agenda is what participating in the arts allows every person to do, whatever their age.

When I visited Mark in the infant school where he is now head, I asked him whether if he had a Year 6 class, with all the pressures that entails, he would still be working in this way. Yes, of course, was his answer, the children deserve nothing less.

References

Alexander, R. J. (2001), *Culture and Pedagogy: International comparisons in primary education*. Oxford; Boston, MA: Blackwell.

Anderson, J. (2017), 'An enquiry into the impact of teaching Shakespeare using rehearsal room techniques on children's writing', Springhead Primary School.

Artmonsky, R. (2006), *The School Prints: A romantic project*. Artmonsky Arts.

Arts Council England (2014), 'The value of arts and culture to people and society: an evidence review', www.artscouncil.org.uk/sites/default/files/download-file/Value_arts_culture_evidence_review.pdf

BBC (2018), 'Ten Pieces', www.bbc.com/teach/ten-pieces

Becker, A. (2017), *The Journey Trilogy*. Somerville, MA: Candlewick Press.

Blake, P. (2009), *Peter Blake's ABC*. London: Tate Publishing.

Blake, Q. (1998), *Clown*. London: Red Fox.

Blake, Q. (2005), *Angel Pavement*. London: Red Fox.

Blake, Q. (2009), Conversation with Joann Sfar, French Institute.

Blake, W. (1794) *Songs of Innocence and of Experience*.

British Council (2013), 'World voice', http://music.britishcouncil.org/projects/world-voice

Burke, C. (2017), 'The arts have a fundamental place in education', *The Guardian*, www.theguardian.com/education/2017/mar/31/the-arts-have-a-fundamental-place-in-education

Carroll, L. (2006), *Alice Through the Looking Glass: And what Alice found there*. Illustrated by Peter Blake. London: Merrell Publishers.

Carroll, L. (2015), *Alice's Adventures in Wonderland: 150th anniversary edition*. Illustrated by Salvador Dalí. Princeton, NJ: Princeton University Press.

Collet, I. and Monfort, M. (2013), *L'École joyeuse et parée*. Paris: Paris Musées.

Dahl, R. (2000), *The Enormous Crocodile*. London: Puffin Books.

Davies, M. (2018), 'Strictly Come Dancing's first live show wins a massive peak audience of 10 million', *Digital Spy*, http://www.digitalspy.com/tv/strictly-come-dancing/news/a866844/strictly-come-dancings-first-live-show-ratings-10-million-peak/

Department for Digital, Culture, Media and Sport (2017), 'Taking part 2016/17: annual child release', London: Her Majesty's Stationery

Office. Crown Copyright. https://www.gov.uk/government/statistics/taking-part-201617-annual-child-release

Department for Education (2011), 'The importance of music: a national plan for music education', London: Her Majesty's Stationery Office. Crown Copyright.

Department for Education (2014), 'National curriculum in England: English programmes of study', London: Her Majesty's Stationery Office. Crown Copyright. https://www.gov.uk/government/publications/national-curriculum-in-england-english-programmes-of-study/national-curriculum-in-england-english-programmes-of-study

Department of Education and Science (1967), 'Children and their primary schools', London: Her Majesty's Stationery Office. Crown Copyright.

Elbow, P. (1998), *Writing with Power*. Oxford; New York, NY: Oxford University Press.

English PEN (2010), 'School Blues: Daniel Pennac in interview with Quentin Blake', https://www.englishpen.org/events/school-blues-daniel-pennac-in-interview-with-quentin-blake/

Escher, M. C. (1989), *Escher on Escher: Exploring the infinite*. New York, NY: Harry N. Abrams.

Froebel, F. (1895), *Friedrich Froebel's Pedagogics of the Kindergarten, Or, His Ideas Concerning the Play and Playthings of the Child*. New York, NY: D. Appleton.

Gladwell, M. (2009), *Outliers: The story of success*. London: Penguin.

Gray, P. (2013), *Free to Learn: Why unleashing the instinct to play will make our children happier, more self-reliant, and better students for life*. New York, NY: Basic Books.

Greenwood Place (2018), 'Briefing no.10', https://www.greenwood.place/news/2018/11/6/briefing-no10

Harbour, V. (2018), 'Feeling distraught 7yo grandson having love of writing battered out of him by school...', Tweet, 4 December, 21:58, https://twitter.com/vanessaharbour/status/1070075017818456066?s=11

Henley, D. (2016), *The Arts Dividend: Why investment in culture pays*. London: Elliott and Thompson.

Hoban, R. (2013), *How Tom Beat Captain Najork and His Hired Sportsmen*. London: Walker Books.

Hockney, D. (2012), *Six Fairy Tales from the Brothers Grimm*. London: Royal Academy of Arts.

Jaggi, M. (2010), 'A life in dance: Akram Khan', *The Guardian*, https://www.theguardian.com/culture/2010/sep/27/akram-khan-dance-life

Jones, J. (2017), 'The drop in museum visitors reveals a nation without aspiration or hope', *The Guardian*, https://www.

theguardian.com/artanddesign/jonathanjonesblog/2017/feb/02/
drop-uk-museum-attendance

Klassen, J. (2014), *This Is Not My Hat*. London: Walker Books.

La Fontaine, J. (2007), *The Complete Fables of Jean de la Fontaine*. Translated by Norman R. Shapiro. Middletown, CT: Wesleyan University Press.

Lopiccolo, R. (2018), 'Five ways to boost reading for pleasure in primary schools', *TES*, https://www.tes.com/news/five-ways-boost-reading-pleasure-primary-schools

Massaro, D. (2015), 'Two different communication genres and implications for vocabulary development and learning to read', http://edsource.org/wp-content/uploads/2015/06/massaroJLR1.pdf

Maury, S. (2014), 'All together now – three evolutionary perks of singing', *The Conversation*, https://theconversation.com/all-together-now-three-evolutionary-perks-of-singing-35367

Monro, H. (1914), *Children of Love*. London: The Poetry Bookshop.

Morpurgo, M. (2014), *On Angel Wings*. London: Egmont.

Nordoff Robbins (2016), 'What is music therapy?', http://www.nordoff-robbins.org.uk/what-is-music-therapy

Norman Ackroyd Meets Robert Macfarlane (2018), BBC Radio 4, 17 October, https://www.bbc.co.uk/programmes/m0000qkv

Oke, J. and Oke, J. (2005), *Naughty Bus*. Budleigh Salterton: Little Knowall Publishing.

O'Keeffe, G. (1926), 'Foreword' in Anderson Galleries Catalogue. New York, NY: Anderson Galleries.

Okri, B. (1997), *A Way of Being Free*. London: Head of Zeus.

Paine, L. (2014), *Complete Guide to Primary Dance*. Leeds: Human Kinetics.

Pennac, D. (2006), *The Rights of the Reader*. Illustrated by Quentin Blake. London: Walker Books.

Pennac, D. (2007), *School Blues*. London: MacLehose Press.

Rattle, S. (2014), 'Simon Rattle: "Learning music is a birthright. And you have to start young".' Interview for *The Guardian*, https://www.theguardian.com/music/2014/aug/31/simon-rattle-interview-proms-learning-music-birthright

Rosen, M. (2004), *Michael Rosen's Sad Book*. London: Walker Books.

Rosen, M. (2016), *What is Poetry?* London: Walker Books.

Rosen, M. (2017), 'Picture books enable children to make cognitive leaps between text and picture…', Tweet, 23 November 2017, 15:42, https://twitter.com/MichaelRosenYes/status/933707239847813121

Rowling, J. K. (1997) *Harry Potter and the Philosopher's Stone*. London: Bloomsbury.

Royal Shakespeare Company (2015), 'How we develop new ideas', www.rsc.org.uk/about-us/how-we-make-theatre/how-we-develop-new-ideas

Royal Shakespeare Company (2016), 'The Learning and Performance Network', www.rsc.org.uk/education/impact-and-research/research-into-our-work/learning-and-performance-network

Royal Shakespeare Company (2018), 'Impact and research', www.rsc.org.uk/education/impact-and-research

Rundell, K. (2013), *Rooftoppers*. London: Faber and Faber.

Samuels, D. (2008), *Kindertransport*. London: Nick Hern Books.

Smith, Mr and Mrs (1977), *The Long Slide*. London: Jonathan Cape.

Stanislavski, C. (2013), *Building a Character*. London: Bloomsbury.

Stevenson, R. L. (1885), *A Child's Garden of Verses*. London: Longhaus, Green and Co.

The Kennedy Center (2018), 'Say it with rhythm! A performance demo with Dr. Nina Kraus featuring Mickey Hart and Zakir Hassain', https://www.youtube.com/watch?v=BE8wuQNWUuM&feature=youtu.be

Trainor, L. (2013), 'The emotional baby: how infants respond to music', Interview for *National Geographic*, https://blog.nationalgeographic.org/2013/11/12/the-emotional-baby-how-infants-respond-to-music/

Turner, C. (2018), 'Shakespeare gives children as young as three a confidence boost, RSC's director of education says', *The Telegraph*, www.telegraph.co.uk/news/2018/02/04/shakespearegives-children-young-three-confidence-boost-rscs/

Wang, J. and Wang, H. (2016), *Cozy Classics: Pride and Prejudice*. San Francisco, CA: Chronicle Books.

Warhol, A. (1958), *The Little Red Hen*. New York, NY: Doubleday.

White, T. H. (1938), *The Sword in the Stone*. London: Collins.

Wiesner, D. (2006), *Flotsam*. New York, NY: Clarion Books.

Wilkinson, B. (2018), 'Why I read aloud to my secondary tutor group', *TES*, www.tes.com/news/why-i-read-aloud-my-secondary-tutor-group?amp&__twitter_impression=true

World Health Organization (2014), 'Mental health: a state of well-being', www.who.int/features/factfiles/mental_health/en/

Index

ABC 18
able children 112
Ackroyd, Norman 12
active learning 29–30
Adams, John 50
ADHD 79
Aldeburgh, Suffolk 55
Alexander, Katie 68, 69, 70, 75
Alexander, Robin 3–4
Alice in Wonderland 18
Alice Through the Looking Glass 18
Andersen, Hans Christian 108
Anderson, Brian 15, 87, 89
Anderson, Jan 90–7
Angel of the North 22
Angel Pavement 41
'Arnolfini Portrait, The' 13–14
arts
  and playing 9–12
  responses to 13–14
  and success 14–15
  and teachers 15–16
Artsmark 3
Atkinson, Delroy 86
audiobooks 101
Auntie's Wood 111

Bacchus and Ariadne 25
Balsom, Alison 50–1
Bang on a Can All-Stars 50
Barber, John 55
Barcombe Primary School, Sussex 41
BBC 48–9
Becker, Aaron 18
'Bed in Summer' (poem) 103
Bellerby, Emma 71
Bettioui, Nadya 79–82
Bhesania, Tess 51, 68–9, 70
Blake, Peter 18
Blake, Quentin 6, 9–10, 11, 15, 18, 19, 41, 106, 107, 108

Blake, William 103–4
Blance, Ellen 106
book-sharing assemblies 110
Braque, Georges 33
Bridge Connection 3
Brill, Patrick 31–2
British Kodály Association 62
Britten, Benjamin 55
Britten-Pears Foundation 55
budgets 3

Cambridge Curiosity and Imagination
  (CCI) 111
  Fantastical Maps model 111–12
Candoco 65
cave paintings 21
Chagrin d'école (*School Blues*) 106
Challenge 59 organisation 75
churches, art in 21
clapping 44
Clark, Emma Chichester 19
Clegg, Alec 4
Cleveland Road Primary School, Ilford
  12, 13, 23, 51, 68–75
Clown 18
collage writing 117
Collins, Anita 59
Condliffe, Kate 89–90
contemporary art and sculpture 22–3, 30
Cook, Ann 106
creative language 111
creativity 11–12, 16, 82, 83, 120
Creed, Martin 33

Dahl, Roald 18
Dalí, Salvador 18
dance 12, 13
  barriers 64–6
  Cleveland Road Primary School, Ilford
    (case study) 68–75
  creative dance 67

within cross-curricular setting 67–8
dance for all 66–8
versus PE 63–4
Daumier, Honoré 19
Deller, Jeremy 33
disability, and dance 64–5
Discovery 51, 53
docents 26
'Don't clap this one back' 44
drama 77–8
   instrumental route 78–82
   intrinsic route 82–5
   inviting theatre companies into school 85
   rehearsals 83
   school production 83
   Springhead Primary School, North Staffordshire (case study) 86–96
   trips to theatres 85–6
drawing skills 21
Drew, Tori 64, 65–8
dyslexia 15

Education Endowment Foundation 79
education policy 3
Elbow, Peter 119, 120
Eliza and the Swans 55
empathy, and drama 98
encouragement 6
Escher, M. C. 12
Eyck, Jan Van 13

Fables 32
fairy tales 108
faith, and dance 65
Feversham Primary Academy, Bradford 55–61, 107, 120
fiction book 110
Fighting Temeraire, The 126
fine artists 17–18
Flotsam 18
Foreman, Michael 19
free art resources 21–3
Frostick, Richard 45–7, 51, 61

galleries 23–5, 30–1
gallery-based education 6
Garland, Tessa 40
Garsington Opera 54–5
Gateshead 22

Gillingham, Karen 55
Giordano, Luca 26–7
Gladwell, Malcolm 11
Gogh, Van 2
Gormley, Antony 22
Gould, Hazel 55
Goya 19
Grafton Primary School, Islington 34–40, 112–21
Gray, Peter 10

Hadow, William 4
Hamilton, Anthea 33
Harbour, Vanessa 112
Hardenberger, Håkan 50
Harry Potter and the Philosopher's Stone 101
Hatoum, Mona 30
Hazzard, Mark 83–4, 123–6
Henley, Darren 4
Hepworth Gallery, 'School Prints' series 32–4
Hepworth Wakefield 31
Histon Children's Centre Footprints project 111
Hoban, Russell 9–10, 11
Hockney, David 17
hotseat interviewing 78
House of Illustration 21
How Tom Beat Captain Najork and His Hired Sportsmen 9–10
human body reading 107

Idrees, Naveed 56–7, 60–1
illustrated books 17–21
imaginative playing 10–11
Immediate Theatre 80
INSET planning session 21, 22
instrumental route, of drama 78–82
instruments 58–9
intrinsic route, of drama 82–5

Jones, Jonathan 24
Journey 18

Khan, Akram 66
Kindertransport 112
King's College London 79
Klassen, Jon 18
'Knife Crime Strategy' 80

132   Index

'Knife Free' initiative 80
Kodály method 58, 62
Kraus, Nina 43

language delay, children with 79
Learning and Performance Network 86
'L'École joyeuse et parée' (exhibition) 32
Léger, Fernand 33
listening
    to children 26–8
    to music 48–50
literature 99–100
    benefits of 102–5
    challenges and consolations 105–10
    Grafton Primary School, Islington (case study) 112–21
    voices 100–1
    writing 110–12
Little Red Hen 18
live music 50–2
London Bubble Theatre 79
London Music Masters 14
London's Old Vic theatre 86
London Symphony Orchestra 53
Long Slide, The 19–21
Lopiccolo, Rachel 109
Lowry, L.S 33

Macbeth 85
map-making 111–12
Marshall, Sybil 4
Marten, Helen 34
Matisse, Henri 33
Maury, Susan 48
Melville, Elena Arévalo 111
Messenger, David 123
Mirza, Haroon 34
Mistry, Dhruva 21
Monro, Harold 104–5
Monster 106–7
more able and talented (MAT) children 112
Morpurgo, Michael 83–4
Musée du Petit Palais 32
museum 23–4
museum fatigue 26
music 111
    'drawing' 50
    Feversham Primary Academy, Bradford (case study) 55–61

instruments 52
learning instruments 58–9
listening 48–50
live music 50–2
responsibility of application of 52–5
rhythm 43–5
singing 45–8
Music Centre London (MCL) 45–6
Music Mark External Services Directory 53

Naidoo, Veena 68
narrative techniques 21
narrative writing 111
Nash, John 33
national cultures 4
National Gallery 6, 14, 18, 24, 25, 31
National Plan for Music Education (NPME) 53
natural sounds 49
Naughty Bus 18
Ndungu, Tonee 76
New Vic Theatre 95
Nordoff–Robbins music therapy 44

Ofsted 3
O'Hanlon, Jacqui 90, 98
Oke, Jan and Jerry 18
Okri, Ben 11–12
On Angel Wings 83–4
One Dance UK 75
operas 54–5
outdoor experiences 111
outdoor sculpture 21
'Overheard on a Saltmarsh' (poem) 104–5
Overy, Katie 59

Paine, Lyn 65
Pankhurst, Sylvia 86
Paris 32
Pears, Peter 55
Pennac, Daniel 106, 107, 110
Perseus Turning Phineas and His Followers to Stone 26–7
PE, versus dance 63–4
photography 23
Picasso, Pablo 33
picture books 21, 40–1
playing, and arts 9–12
Plowden, Bridget 4

Index **133**

poetry 102–5, 110
'Poison Tree, A' (poem) 103–4
Pride and Prejudice 18
primary school memory 1–2, 4–6
process drama 78
PSHCE (personal, social, health and citizenship education) 21
public libraries 109
public performance 50–1
public statues 21
Pyne, Andrea 44

Rawnsley, Brenda 33
Read, Herbert 4, 33
recording sounds 49–50
resources 60, 62
rhythm 43–5
Riddell, Chris 18
Rights of the Reader, The 107–8
Robinson, Ken 4
Rooftoppers 70
Rosen, Michael 2, 18, 102
Rotheram, Jimmy 57–60, 62
Round House Primary Academy, The 109, 111
Rowling, J.K. 101
Royal Shakespeare Company (RSC) 85–6, 86–7, 97, 98
Royal Society of Arts 79
Rubens, Peter Paul 48
Rundell, Katherine 70

Samuels, Diane 112
school, as reading community 109–10
Semele 5
Shakespearean dramas 86–96, 98
shared singing experience 48
singing 45–8
Sing Up 48
Six Fairy Tales from the Brothers Grimm 17
Smith, Bob and Roberta 31–2
Smith, Ray 19
sociodramatic play 10
soundless animation 111
soundscape 49
Speech Bubbles programme 79
Springhead Primary School, North Staffordshire 15, 86–96

statues 5, 21
Stevenson, Robert Louis 103
Strictly Come Dancing 63
Sword in the Stone, The 125
Sylvia 86

Take One Picture scheme 6
team walk 22–3
teamwork 83
'Tell Me a Picture' (exhibition) 6, 18–19
Ten Pieces (BBC) 49
text-less picture book 111
This Is Not My Hat 18
3D art element 31
Topolski, Feliks 33
Trainor, Laurel 43, 45
Turner, J.M.W. 2, 48

Varèse, Edgard 50
verbal and visual skills 15
visual arts 48
    Grafton Primary School, Islington (case study) 34–40
    illustration 17–21
    making most of 40–1
    noticing 21–3
    school as art gallery 31–40
    visiting art spaces 23–31
voices 100–1, 120
Voices Foundation 62

wall painting 22
Warhol, Andy 18
wellbeing, and dance 67
'Where'er You Walk' 5
Whitworth Gallery 31
Wiesner, David 18
Windmill Hill Primary School 123–6
Winehouse, Amy 2
Wootton Bassett Infants' School, Wiltshire 83, 107
World Health Organization 67
World Voice 46
Wylie, Rose 34

Yorkshire Sculpture Park 22, 31–2

Zumpe, Suzi 55